Running With Your Second Wind

Phillip Corbett

Running With Your Second Wind

Phillip Corbett

Evergreen
PRESS

Mobile, Alabama

Running With Your Second Wind
by Phillip Corbett
Copyright ©2013 Phillip Corbett

Cover design by C.J. McDaniel

Second printing, 2015

ISBN 978-1-58169-472-7
For Worldwide Distribution
Printed in the U.S.A.

Evergreen Press
P.O. Box 191540 • Mobile, AL 36619
800-367-8203

Contents

Acknowledgments

The Tip of the Iceberg

There are so many to thank who have made this book possible. The first is my beautiful wife, Rachel, who has made it easy to hear God and allow me to live my God-given dream. She releases me on a regular basis, even when she is not able to travel with me, to touch the lives of others.

Johnny Knight, has insisted I write my story and the principles I have learned. I never thought what I had inside of me might really help other people. His hunger for the presence of God has only fueled my own. He has taken so much time from his own life and personal ministry to travel with me and keep my hands lifted upwards.

I am indebted to the pastors, who have allowed me in their pulpit and trusted me with their sheep; to the individuals who have spent many hours, helping me edit my manuscript—Ann Powell, Connie Wright, Donnie Pate, Lisa Myers, Rachel Corbett, and Tom Wymore; and to the individuals who gave me permission to share their testimonies.

I would like to add a very special thanks to a dear friend Tom Donnan—it was not chance that brought our lives together. To Pastors Glenn and Mary Hammack from Andrews, Texas. Without each of you, this book never would have happened.

When Rachel and I moved to Corrigan in 1985, we met two special women of faith; Lydia Wright, and her daughter-in-law Charlotte. These women and their families have been the nucleus and strength of our church from the beginning. We have enjoyed working with five generations who continue to serve God and because of them I often say, "My future is looking pretty good."

Rachel and I are blessed to be the pastors of such a wonderful group of people. Their passion for Christ, coupled with their love for people, allow them to enjoy the pleasure of helping others experience greater things in God. I am released on a regular basis to share the message of revival with other pastors and congregations. I realize that I am only "The tip of the iceberg;" I may be the one speaking but I represent a whole lot of other great people back home.

Foreword

Several years ago an evangelist friend of mine called me from Texas. He wanted to tell me about the revival service he had sat in the night before in a little town in East Texas. He excitedly proclaimed, "I think this is the real thing." As a result of that phone call, I placed a call to Phil Corbett, pastor of the church. For over 90 minutes he shared stories of what they were experiencing. That 90-minute conversation was the first of many conversations, emails, and Facebook exchanges. As an evangelist who has preached nearly 40 revival meetings that went beyond the planned time and some of which have been described as the greatest meetings in the history of the Church, I am interested in the real thing.

Since that phone call, Phil and I have shared a common pulpit at conferences and summits on revival. I have preached in his church. We have co-hosted events geared to assist pastors and churches pursuing revival. We have thoroughly thrashed through many issues relating to revival.

I recommend this book to two types of readers. This book will be of great value to the pastor of the average church who is hungry for a move of God. My library is full of books on revival. Many are written by scholars years after the fact. Others are theoretical treatises written by people who have never experienced genuine revival. I have found the above books to have value, but they leave out important areas. This book is written by a pastor who has experienced the real thing and is written close enough to the outpouring to recall important steps. At the same time it has enough distance to give some objectivity. Phil is one of most "feet on the ground" people I have met. I found the material theologically sound and immediately practical.

The second reader I think will benefit is the average believer. The fact that Phil is a pastor cannot be missed. His message consistently speaks to the average person in the average church. As I read the manuscript, my mind was drawn to people I am currently ministering to who would find the material to be of great help in their personal walk with God. I love the home spun illustrations from life in East Texas.

The stories have reminded me of the technique of a storyteller from Galilee who changed the world. The author's application of biblical stories and phrases to real life situations is very good. At times I have thought, "I wish I had said that."

It has been my privilege to preach what I have been told are the longest single church/same evangelist meetings in the history of modern New Zealand. One of those meetings went 20 weeks and was viewed by pastors in Hutt Valley as vital in their journey toward city transformation. The second went 19 weeks in another city. As I write this Foreword, I have just finished 22 months of meetings at a church in Indiana. Phil Corbett has shared many of the principles I have observed in these revivals and wished I could have passed along to those passionate about the Presence of the Lord.

Thanks Phil for leaving your beloved East Texas woods long enough to open your heart to other leaders and followers of Jesus who are hungry for revival. I will be passing this book along to them.

Michael Livengood
Founder and President of Mike Livengood Ministries
Founder and President of Doorkeepers New Zealand.
www.doorkeepers.co.nz
Danville, Illinois and Lower Hutt, New Zealand

Introduction

And suddenly there came a sound from heaven as of a rushing mighty wind (Acts 2:2).

The United States and nations of the world are in need of true revival. We do not need just a series of meetings or extended services but a return of the tangible presence of God wherever believers are gathered. Many people feel frustrated with "church as usual" and have acquired a holy desperation for His Spirit to again fill our sanctuaries.

This book will encourage those who are willing to go beyond the point where nominal Christians choose to dwell. I speak often of the two places most believers can be found. Using the Old Testament Tabernacle as a reference point, the first place is the outer court, which is a place of merely being converted. The second is known as the inner court, which is an inner chamber, representing God's power and presence. I write this book for those who wish to press into and live in the inner chamber, or what I refer to as the presence of God.

We do not need another book of someone's opinion or theory. This book is filled with proven principles I discovered after countless hours of pursuing His presence, which have produced fruit in my life personally and in my ministry. These principles, which are reinforced with testimonies, can also work for you. They are true whether you are a seasoned pastor who longs for something more, a worship leader who desires a more intimate song, or a lay member who is ready to go deeper.

My wife, as well as friends in ministry, have encouraged me to write down the things I have learned and the miracles I have seen as a result of practicing what I am about to share. This book is simple enough that a child could understand it, yet deep enough to challenge the mature believer. In each chapter, you will find stories that will inspire and encourage you and provoke your hunger as you begin your own pursuit of His presence.

In June 1996, God powerfully touched my life at the Brownsville Revival, in Pensacola, Florida. I felt that I had gone as far as I could go in ministry, and then I had a powerful encounter with God there. Since that time, the congregation I pastor in Corrigan, Texas, has enjoyed three extended revivals, and my life and ministry have changed dramatically. My congregation now releases me on a regular basis to carry the flames of revival out from this small East Texas town.

My ministry outside of my local church is known as "Second Wind Ministries" and has a general focus on three different groups of believers. The first group I address is all believers in general because each one needs a second chapter of Acts experience, which is commonly referred to as being filled with the Holy Spirit. After receiving this infilling, spiritual fruit will be produced, new gifts will be developed, and effective ministries will be birthed.

The second group I speak to are the many pastors who are feeling burned out and ready to quit their ministry. Because I too, at one point in my life, experienced frustration, I know well the feelings of being discouraged, disappointed, and feeling like a failure. I had to pick myself up, shake the dust off, and pursue God again. God is now allowing me to enjoy life and ministry with the same passion I experienced at the beginning. This renewal happened after I received my "second wind."

The third group I am speaking to are churches, the corporate bodies of believers, who are hungry for fruitful, effective ministry that only happens in His presence. Many churches have appeared to have lost ground over the past few years, but God is preparing a re-energized Church to emerge; one like the world has never seen. I believe God has saved His best for last, and the Church as a whole is about to run with her second wind. God is positioning entire congregations, small and large, people just like you and me, to usher in a last days revival of global proportions. Large churches and international ministries are not the only ones who are called to successfully fulfill all that Christ told us to do. God is not going to overlook you because you may not appear to be as gifted and talented as others, or because the place you are called to serve may be in an out of the way place.

In this book, you will be reminded why we need His presence. You will read principles on how to attract His presence, what happens when His presence comes, and how to keep His presence. You will read testimonies of persons who have been saved, healed, and delivered after a powerful encounter with God. I have seen lives changed, pastors transformed, churches re-ignited, and communities impacted.

I believe the greatest testimonies are yet to be seen and the most effective ministries are about to be birthed. I trust you will enjoy these stories and glean from the principles I share, as much as I was blessed by living them. Get ready! You are about to run with your second wind!

Chapter One

Roll Out the Barrels

Elijah said unto Ahab, get thee up, eat and drink; for there is the sound of abundance of rain (1 Kings 18:41).

People seem to be tired of the term "revival," but it seems to be the one word most people understand and connect with the moving of the Holy Spirit. I am anticipating a revival of global proportions. Revivals have been observed affecting churches, cities, and entire regions, but one of global proportions is yet to be seen.

Every time I read the following scripture, hope rises up inside me because I believe, based on scripture, the tide is about to turn. Could it be that both America and Europe are going to experience a move of God similar to that which is seen in South America, Africa, and parts of Asia?

> *Come, and let us return unto the LORD: for he hath torn, and he will heal us; he hath smitten, and he will bind us up. After two days will he revive us: in the third day he will raise us up, and we shall live in his sight. Then shall we know, if we follow on to know the LORD: his going forth is prepared as the morning; and he shall come unto us as the rain, as the latter and former rain unto the earth* (Hosea 6:1-3).

This passage brings to light several interesting things. Hosea states that God will break us so He can mend us. Many Christians are off course, and the only way God can fix them is to start new. He will break

1

us, which never feels good; but the brokenness leads to a new beginning, making it worth all the pain.

After two days He will revive us: in the third day He will raise us up, and we shall live in His sight (Hosea 6:2).

For two thousand years, the Church has been somewhat weak and often ineffective. The scripture states that with the Lord, a thousand years is as a day. It was on the third day Jesus arose from His grave. I believe the third millennia is the time for His Body to arise from sleep. After two days, He will revive us, but on the third day, He will raise us up. Living in His sight suggests living in His presence under an open heaven.

One of the first things recorded about God in the Bible was that He "moved." In Genesis chapter one it says, "The Spirit of God moved on the face of the deep," and so it will be in the end times. God will continue to move.

I believe the last days revival is, as some would say, "a done deal," and it is only a matter of time before His plan unfolds. Hosea says it is "prepared as the morning." Until God's timetable requires no more sun, moon, or stars, the sun will continue to rise in the morning. Just as we know the sun will rise again tomorrow, there must be a last days revival. We know that God keeps His Word, and an outpouring is "prepared as the morning."

I do not believe that God in His mercy would let a nation that has been steeped in the gospel be destroyed until He provides an opportunity to repent. Historically America and Europe have been a beacon of light and hope to the world for the past two hundred years, and soon I believe God will begin wooing them back to Himself.

Moses spoke of the desire in the heart of God by saying,

"... as truly as I live, all the earth shall be filled with the glory of the LORD" (Numbers 14:21).

Paul said in Ephesians 5:27,

That he might present it to himself a glorious church.

How can He present to Himself a "glorious Church" if there is no evidence of His presence? God's Word can be trusted regarding a last days revival and the presence of a glory-filled church.

He shall come unto us as the rain, as the latter and former rain unto the earth (Hosea 6:3).

Hosea is clear that a last days revival is coming. "He shall come unto us as the rain." In scripture, rain was often withheld from Israel when the nation walked away from God. Once the people repented, God would again send the rain.

Many people embrace what God once did but are opposed to what He wants to do today. When this new rain begins to fall, it could possibly be unlike anything we have ever seen. Because some Christians are not receptive to something new, God says He will send together the former and the latter rain.

The Church should position itself much like a surfer, waiting for the next big wave. A surfer turns his back from land, paddling away from the shore, gazing into the distance for a wave that appears to be building. Before he catches the wave that he has been waiting for, he must let a lot of insignificant ones pass beneath him. Once he sees the wave he is looking for, he turns to shore and paddles toward it with all his might.

And all the people saw the thunderings, and the lightnings, and the noise of the trumpet, and the mountain smoking: and when the people saw it, they removed, and stood afar off. And they said unto Moses, Speak thou with us, and we will hear: but let not God speak with us, lest we die. And Moses said unto the people, Fear not: for God is come to prove you, and that his fear may be before your faces, that ye sin not. And the people stood afar off, and Moses drew near unto the thick darkness where God was (Exodus 20:18-21).

Moses discovered that the people, like many today, would rather stay where they were comfortable. The children of Israel told Moses it was okay for him to go up the mountain to where God was. As a matter of fact they told Moses, "Why don't you go up and hear and then you can come tell us what God is saying." Moses did go up into the presence alone. Like Moses you may even be criticized and labeled as being weird. Family, friends, and even some church members may not understand your hunger or why you do the things you do. Sometimes one's own family and even those closest to them will not go along. In our pursuit of His presence, we might find we lost friends on one level but gained new ones on a different level.

When my congregation first began to feel the rivers of refreshing revival, many people experienced unique manifestations. Excited about what God was doing in our lives, I shared what was happening with a neighboring pastor. This elderly man was near retirement age and had served God faithfully for many years. Once I began to share what we were seeing, he simply crossed his arms, chuckled, and cut me off by saying, "Son, I have seen all that God has ever done." His quick response and the attitude he presented somewhat surprised me. Though I did not say it out loud, I thought to myself, *There stands one blind man.* His body language said it all before a word ever came from his mouth. He wasn't really interested in hearing about this new thing God was doing. My heart aches for those who are so closed-minded and refuse to even listen to reports about the new waves of His glory.

Now let us take a portion of the above scripture and go one step further. The word "if" is a very simple word that in itself does not mean much. It is found in verse 3.

> *Then shall we know **if** we follow on to know the Lord* (Hosea 6:3, author emphasis).

"If" is a powerful word that leads one to believe that there is a choice in the matter and precedes following on to know the Lord. When we follow on to know Him, we find there is so much more than what we thought we knew. We need to get out of our little box of believing He can only be what we have personally experienced and can explain. First Corinthians 2:9-10 refers to the deep, unexplainable things of God.

> *But as it is written, Eye hath not seen, nor ear heard, neither have entered into the heart of man, the things which God hath prepared for them that love him. But God hath revealed them unto us by his Spirit:*

for the Spirit searcheth all things, yea, the deep things of God (1 Corinthian 2:9-10).

Isaiah mentions that one day God will do a "new thing."

Remember ye not the former things, neither consider the things of old. Behold, I will do a new thing; now it shall spring forth; shall ye not know it? I will even make a way in the wilderness, and rivers in the desert (Isaiah 43:18-19).

We are in the "between" of what He just did and what He is about to do. One will never get to the new wave of His glory unless he continues on.

A good way to visualize this is to understand a little about the tabernacle in the Old Testament. Once a man entered through the gates of the tabernacle, he proceeded into the outer court. There were two pieces of furniture there and both were made of solid brass. When brass is mentioned in the scriptures, it represents judgment. The first piece of furniture that the priest encountered was the brazen altar, which was the place of sacrifice. The second furnishing was the brazen laver, literally a wash basin. This basin represented water baptism and newness of life. The symbols here represent having your sins forgiven and following the Lord's command to be baptized in water. These actions may be enough to keep someone out of hell and get them into heaven, but they don't provide any spiritual power for living.

Most churches are in fact what can be called "outer court" churches. These churches are content with getting people saved and baptized but fail to bring them into a deeper experience. God did not give Moses instruction for pews so this is not to be seen as a place to stop. Two choices are presented—the first is to stay content where you are and the second choice is to go forward. The first choice is not a place of spiritual dynamics or growth, only a place where one is changed.

During their time of service, the priests moved from the outer court into the inner court. Once inside the door, the priests saw that everything had changed from brass to pure gold. Gold in the scriptures represents reward. Any priest choosing to continue would approach the table of shewbread, which was a place to meet with God face to face. The priests were responsible every Sabbath day to replace the twelve loaves of bread with fresh ones. It was natural hunger for the bread and the spiritual hunger for God that brought men through the door to a place of fellowship and intimacy.

There were no instructions given to Aaron about what the proper protocol was to be for coming into the inner court. Each priest was allowed to choose—either he could move toward the table prepared with bread or to the candlestick that burned with oil. The candlestick represented the power and enlightening of the Holy Spirit. It is in the light of the Holy Spirit that men are empowered for daily living and where spiritual gifts and fruit are produced.

The third piece of furniture was the altar of incense, which suggests intercession. The priest would enter past the veil into the most holy place. This information is not to give you a lesson on the tabernacle, but to point out things in the inner court that would never be experienced unless a priest made the choice to press in.

People are given a choice to either stay where they are or go forward in God. Going forward requires change, which is something people dislike and are naturally resistant to. Most people hang onto the traditions they are familiar with, growing stagnant and cold, instead of pressing in to fresh manna from heaven.

My observation is that most Christians prefer the style of music, ministry, or preaching of the period when they had their first experience with God. Unless a person yields himself to the working of the Holy Spirit, he may not have the ability or desire to receive something new. People are often convinced that anything other than what they have personally seen cannot possibly be from God.

There are choices every believer is allowed to make. One such choice is to stay where they are or press on to a new season that God has prepared. After Moses' death, Joshua, their new leader, and the children of Israel were confronted with the Jordan River. With this apparent obstacle in front of them, God sent a message that everything was about to change.

The children of Israel knew they had to cross the Jordan River in order to receive their inheritance. The Lord did not give them a choice—He gave them a command. Now Israel had two choices: believe what Joshua told them God had said or keep serving and worshipping God in the same manner as they had with Moses during the previous forty years. Crossing the Red Sea into the wilderness meant life to them when they came out of Egypt, but staying where life once was on that same side of the Jordan River now meant certain death.

Isn't it funny how a new way can quickly become an old way and how the things we once struggled to resist are the things we now struggle to maintain. When Moses brought Israel out of Egypt, the people, though they enjoyed their new freedom, began to grumble and complain, wanting to go back to Egypt. Forty years later, would the same nation of people choose to stay where they were and keep what they had or cross over? Of course, they were ready for homes, land, crops, and to live in the city; but it would also mean that God would manifest His presence in a brand new way.

No longer would Israel be led by the pillar and cloud. Now, they would actually be following men. The priests were the ones to carry the ark on their shoulders, and the people were to follow. The people had shown they could follow a cloud, but could they follow men?

And they commanded the people, saying, When ye see the ark of the covenant of the LORD your God, and the priests the Levites bearing it, then ye shall remove from your place, and go after it. Yet there shall be a space between you and it, about two thousand cubits by measure: come not near unto it, that ye may know the way by which ye must go: for ye have not passed this way heretofore. And Joshua said unto the people, Sanctify yourselves: for tomorrow the LORD will do wonders among you (Joshua 3:3-5).

This was a radically different set of instructions from what was followed while in the wilderness listening to Moses. They were told to "go after it" and follow the ark, even though they had never seen it done like that or travelled down this particular path before. Once the people decided to trust God, leaving the wilderness and the understanding of the way that God had moved behind them, a new promise was given to them, "Tomorrow, the Lord will do wonders among you." You can maintain a "yesterday" mentality if you desire, but I choose to follow God, wherever and however He leads. As a young pastor, I had to unlearn as many things as I had to learn, and this meant being stretched. If a man wants to be on the cutting edge of what God is going to do, allowing Him to change us is the price one must pay. A man must allow himself to be taken down an unfamiliar path. If you trust Him today, you can be assured that tomorrow you will see what you have never seen before.

To support my family during the early years of ministry in Corrigan, I worked at a local supermarket. This was a strategic place to work because I came to know almost everyone in town on a first name basis. I once had a well meaning lady come to me and say, "If your church would be like all the other churches in town, everyone would want to come to it." Sounds like a pretty good thought if I was into the church growth mindset. After the Lord touched my life, I made a decision that I would never be "people driven" but rather "presence driven." While being people driven might attract others, being presence driven attracts Him.

As a pastor, I had to let good people slip through my hands and great ideas pass me by, only because they were not going in the same direction I was called to go. I am not saying I severed friendships or burned bridges, but I had to realize not every person in Corrigan was looking for the same thing out of a church as I was looking for. It was okay that my church was not the biggest in town, but in exchange, God brought people into my life as hungry for His presence as I was.

I made a choice to pursue Him. This was taking a risk because if I pursued what I thought attracted Him rather than attracting them, and His presence didn't come, then I would look like a fool. I believed if I could attract Him, then His presence alone would attract others. People suggested that if I wanted to attract a crowd, I should sing from the hymnal rather than from "off the wall." I was told if we would sing what people prefer, a Southern traditional style, people would feel comfortable; or if we didn't sing so much, people would come. It is funny that what they call singing, we called worship. I also believed that people should be committed to the House of God and prayer meetings as well as being challenged to more than Sunday morning Christianity. Corrigan didn't need another church that was like the others. If what I was being told worked, I wondered why the other churches were not filled with people. I enjoy fellowship with other churches and their pastors are dear friends, but even though you know you are different theologically, there is pressure to conform in methods. I was willing to try something new. I was determined that if the new thing did not work, we could go back to what was not working before.

Let me refer back to the story of Elijah and the prophets of Baal in 1 Kings 18. Elijah gave a challenge that the "God who answered by fire would be the true and living God of Israel." Those worshipping Baal cried out all day, even cutting themselves, but Baal never responded. After Elijah rebuilt the altar of the Lord and placed the sacrifice on top, he had men bring twelve barrels of water, and he soaked the sacrifice. To ensure the water did not run off, a trench was dug around the perimeter of the stones. After praying, the fire of God came from heaven and completely consumed the water-drenched sacrifice, the wood, the stones and even the dust, leaving absolutely nothing unburned.

The question I had often wondered was why the twelve barrels of water? Why not ten or even thirteen barrels? Many scholars feel the twelve barrels represented the twelve tribes of Israel. That probably is what it means, but I like to think that it could have been all the water they had left. It had not rained in Israel in over three years, and there was not even dew on the ground. The rivers had dried up and the cisterns were empty. All the water they had left was in the barrels for safekeeping. It was here that Elijah took his own risk. If he emptied out all the barrels, there would be no water left. If he trusted God and poured out all the water they had, would God give them more in the form of rain?

I believe the major obstacle in embracing a fresh move of God is we have too much water in reserve from the last thing God did. The water in the barrels by this time had to have become stagnant. Can we believe that if God poured out His Spirit once, He could pour it out again?

I am an avid outdoorsman. Every year, my freezers are filled with vegetables I have grown or meat I have killed and processed myself. Before planting a new garden or beginning a new hunting season, if I did not share with others the vegetables from my last harvest and meat from my last hunt, I would not have room for a fresh supply of food I was preparing to receive. The only thing that would convince me to empty out the old is the belief that something new and fresh was coming.

Keeping things new and fresh is also illustrated in the Old Testament rituals of the priests. Twice a day the priests went into the inner court and trimmed the wicks and removed the ashes from the candlestick. If the priests failed to do this, the ashes from the old flame would extinguish the present one. The Lord had given them instructions that it should be a perpetual flame and was never to go out. Once the wicks were trimmed, the ashes were taken outside the camp and buried. Don't let the fire burning inside you yesterday be the thing that puts out your fire today. The biggest threat to the next thing God does is the last thing He did.

Remember the one word that was the key word found in Hosea 6:3? That word is "if." "If we follow on to know the Lord, his going forth is prepared as the morning, and he shall come unto us as the latter and the former rain unto the earth."

Please do not stop your pursuit of His presence. Your risk will pay off huge dividends if you turn loose of what used to be and prepare to embrace what He is about to do.

Elijah kept sending his servant to look for any kind of sign that it was about to rain. Keep in mind, what you are looking for is by faith; your efforts and your journey are in faith. You are looking for what you know is there but just has not manifested itself yet. After many attempts, the servant reported a cloud about the size of a man's hand, which was all Elijah needed to hear, and the race was on.

> *Elijah said unto Ahab, get thee up, eat and drink; for there is a sound of abundance of rain.... And it came to pass that the heaven was black with clouds and wind, and there was a great rain* (1 Kings 18:41, 45).

Even though Elijah had not seen it, he could see it. Even though he had not felt a single raindrop, he had already been drenched. Although the Spirit does not appear to be moving, some can see it stirring. Although the revival we are preparing for has not yet come, some may already be walking in it. Always thank God for what He did, but get ready to embrace what He desires to do. Get ready to run with your "Second Wind."

Chapter Two

Two Thousand Horses

I will give thee two thousand horses, if thou be able on thy part to set riders upon them (Isaiah 36:8).

Members of my church seem to have always enjoyed pursuing the presence of God. Groups of them have often traveled with me to revivals anytime the opportunity was presented. During this pursuit, it didn't matter what church we attended or who the speaker was, different ones with me were called out of the crowd and given prophetic words. Evangelists, pastors, and prophets each told us to prepare ourselves because they could see revival coming. These men and women who spoke into our lives may not have known each other, but the messages they shared were always the same. During times of intercessory prayer at church, prophetic utterances would also come from our own members declaring the same message. There were prophetic words for the corporate body, and on a more personal level, what God would do with our lives and ministry.

Prophetic utterances we received during prayer meetings told of the crowds of people who would eventually attend our services, the global impact that would come, and the specific distances some would travel. Other prophetic words mentioned there would be an "explosion in ministry," we would "minister to the nations," that "our hunger would be known around the world," and we would become "a fertile environment for bringing up sons and daughters in ministry."

Until the prophetic words actually came to pass, I often wondered,

"Why on earth would such a big God use such a small congregation in this East Texas sawmill town?" Outside East Texas, few people have ever heard of Corrigan with a population of less than 1,600 people.

If you believe God has given you a promise, you should prepare to run with it. James 2:20 says, "Faith without works is dead." If you are truly convinced the word is true, don't just wait for it to happen. Prepare yourself for what you believe is actually coming. Most do not understand the physical, emotional, and financial demands that a move of God requires. I have come to understand that a true move of God doesn't just happen.

Jeremiah 12:5 states, "If thou hast run with the footmen, and they have wearied thee, then how canst thou contend with horses?" If it is all a man can do to drag himself out of bed and go to church on Sunday morning, how on earth can he say he is ready for the greater things of God? If merely keeping up with other people becomes a challenge to him, how can he run with the horses?

There will always be a higher level in God than where you are. Some men are merely walking, others may be walking in an anointing, and still others are operating in a realm called "glory." If normal things in life and ministry challenge a man, how can he boast he wants to see greater things? Running with the footmen would represent one having an anointing or a gifting in his life. If a man finds this to be a challenge, how can he keep up with those who have found a way to operate on a higher level that can be described as running with the horses?

People often pray for a greater anointing or for gifts to develop in their lives and ministry. The anointing is to be desired, even treasured; but if one is not careful, the focus can be put on oneself and what one does.

The anointing carries a reference to oil, which is able to make a person glisten or shine. Which is greater, a man that shines when the anointing comes upon him or the things that happen when he removes himself out of the way and lets God's glory move in? Under the anointing, a man looks better than he actually is. When the glory comes, it completely obscures the man because it is the very presence of God.

If they are not careful, men would prefer the anointing level because it could cause people to look at *them* and desire the thing which is flowing from them, such as a word they can give or the impartation they bring when they lay hands on others. When the glory falls, God works and we can only stand back in awe. We watch the miracles begin to happen, and man has nothing to do with it.

There is always a higher level, which is the reason one must press forward. I quote again from Hosea 6, "…if we follow on to know the Lord." A man can choose to remain where he is or climb to a higher level.

On several occasions, I have taken groups from my church to the First Assembly of God Church in Phoenix, Arizona, and Pastor Tommy Barnett's Pastor School. One of the highlights of these trips was to take a climb to the top of Prayer Mountain. This mountain is located immediately behind the sanctuary on the same property as the church. The summit provides a commanding view of the church property and the entire city of Phoenix. Every year during Pastors' School, people are encouraged to let God reveal His plan for their lives. After God speaks to hearts during the training sessions, people are encouraged to make the trek to the summit, spending time in prayer.

I have made the trek on each trip to the summit of Prayer Mountain. During one of these excursions, I made ten observations about people and climbing, which can be an analogy for someone going from an anointing level to walking in the glory of God.

- Not everyone wants to go to the top.
- Some are content to watch others go up the mountain.
- Many people refuse to go by themselves.
- Some are not dressed for climbing and boots seem to work better than dress shoes.
- To climb, a person must have the proper equipment.
- People go as far as their level of commitment takes them.
- People don't always set aside the time they need to climb.
- The higher one goes, the harder the climb becomes.
- There are fewer beaten paths the closer one gets to the summit.
- People might need others to lend a hand to pull them over the top.

I have made up my mind to be on the cutting edge of whatever I do for God. If I climb the mountain, I am determined to be the first man to the summit.

While walking in the anointing, men walk on a level where so much rests on them. In an unhealthy way, some men need people to need them, to need their ministry, to need their gift, or to receive from their anointing. Back to the analogy of horses, a foot soldier can become exhausted very quickly while carrying out an order in battle. The weight of his armor and the weapons and provisions he must carry can be physically demanding. When he is on his feet, he can only go as far as his own strength can carry him.

If a soldier on foot can make a transition and become a horse soldier, he will become much more effective. When a rider becomes one with the horse, he will draw strength from it. The horseman can carry a much heavier load, travel much quicker, and go further distances than the soldier just on foot. The soldier on the horse sits higher and can see further than the man on the ground and is never at a disadvantage when others challenge him.

Are you able to walk in a greater dimension? The difference from where you may be to where you could be is the same as comparing a foot soldier and a horseman. The thing most needed in the Kingdom of God is men who draw from the strength of the horse rather than from their own strength. When men learn to walk in the glory, rather than in the anointing, amazing things will begin to happen.

All of us are called to walk on a higher level than where we are, so we must begin preparing ourselves. One should condition himself and receive instructions from others in order to be trained and ready when the opportunity comes.

Sennacherib, King of the Assyrians, approached the small tribe of Judah, not for war but for a military exercise. He needed to keep his soldiers and horsemen sharp and in a state of readiness. He needed an army that would present only a small challenge to his elite forces. The tribe of Judah did not have an adequate military force to defend itself and was the perfect opponent for the Assyrians. In order to give Judah somewhat of a fighting chance, Sennacherib made them a generous offer. If Judah could train men to ride and fight on horses, he would give them two thousand horses to defend themselves.

I will give thee two thousand horses, if thou be able on thy part to set riders upon them (Isaiah 36:8).

I believe the Lord is saying that if a man can show Him he can ride a horse, He will give him a horse. There are insights God chooses to reveal but only to those who are able to make the transition from walking in an anointing to riding in the glory.

The Lord is instructing the Church that if you can make a transition, you can walk in a dimension greater than an anointing. If we can show Him we can ride the horse, He will provide the horses. If we prepare ourselves and learn how to mount the horse and hang on, the Church can transition into more than just a lighthouse. The Lord intends for His House to be a center not only for salvation, but also deliverance and healing.

Sennacherib never was able to perform military maneuvers against Judah. During the night, an angel of the Lord came into the camp of the Assyrians, and 185,000 soldiers and horsemen were killed.

I sensed God was telling me in the time leading up to our revival that I must prepare the congregation. We began pursuing fervently the presence of God, and we prepared for what we thought a sovereign move of God might look like and feel like. I was convinced our opportunity was coming, so I sought out pastors who had been where I felt the Lord was taking us, gleaning all the insight and wisdom I could.

God gave me instructions to develop leaders and train key people in my church. I also received insights that would direct my decisions for my personal life. My wife and I had purchased a small house and major renovations were needed for my family. The Lord gave me instructions to finish projects I was involved in and gave me a timeline, allowing the time I needed to complete the project as well as time for family and personal renewal. These instructions were etched in my spirit the way a man would draw a blueprint. Somehow I knew that all of my preparation was about to lead me into a fruitful season.

David, as a young man, was anointed by Samuel to be the next king over Israel. Though he was chosen to be the next king, he did not leave the green pastures for the palace. After his anointing, he went back to the sheep his father had entrusted to him in the field because there were years of preparation ahead of him. God will never use a man or woman until he or she is fully prepared. David was not ready for the throne, nor was God finished with Saul. David knew he was called to the Kingdom, and he prepared for his destiny by continuing to be faithful taking orders from his father, guarding sheep, and writing songs. While David thought he was only keeping his father's sheep safe from the bear and a lion, God was actually preparing him for a much more formidable foe.

Has God given you a promise? Are you convinced the promise will truly come to pass? He will not bring you into your destiny until you have been properly trained and are ready. Waiting time is not wasted time so take full advantage of all the things He is trying to teach you. Though you think you may be ready, only He knows. He is getting you ready to ride a horse.

Chapter Three

How To Ride a Horse

His horses are swifter than eagles (Jeremiah 4:13).

At least once in their lives, most people have experienced the rush of riding a horse at a full gallop. There is nothing as exhilarating as the sound of the hooves pounding the ground, the flexing of the muscles beneath the saddle, or the feel of the wind in your face.

Riding horses can be a wonderful form of exercise and a great family activity. Horses aren't used for farming or as a means of transportation much anymore, but they can provide someone with a wonderful form of relaxation. For the one who utilizes the horse while at work, the horse will increase their speed, strength, and overall productivity.

I heard about a young man from the city who had his first attempt at riding a horse. He thought it would not be very difficult, even though he had no lessons or prior experience. He mounted the horse unassisted, and it immediately sprang into motion. It galloped along at a steady and rhythmic pace, but then the young man began to slip from the saddle. In terror, he reached for the horse's mane but could not get a firm grip. He tried to throw his arms around the horse's neck, but he slid down the side of the horse anyway. The horse galloped along, seemingly impervious to its slipping rider. Finally, giving up his frail grip, he leaped away from the horse to try and throw himself to safety. Unfortunately, his foot had become entangled in the stirrup, and he was at the mercy of the horse's pounding hooves as his head struck the ground over and over. He was mere moments away from unconsciousness when to his great fortune, the manager from inside the local grocery store saw him, rushed to his aid, and unplugged the carousel.

I want to share with those who have never ridden a horse how they can learn to ride. More than a lesson on riding a horse, I want to show that it is possible to walk on a higher level with God. There is another dimension that Jesus spoke of which enables men to do things greater than Him.

He that believeth on me, the works that I do shall he do also; and greater works than these shall he do (John 14:12).

As long as a man is satisfied where he is, he most likely will feel no need for change. If a man is willing to make changes and grow, he will have a most interesting and fulfilling life. The turning point in my life came when I became tired of where I was and decided I needed to grow.

My journey that led me into greater things in God began a number of years ago when I prayed a very simple prayer that drastically changed my life. The prayer included these words, "Lord, I am so tired of someone else having all the good stories to tell. Would You please give me some of my own?" The stories I wished to tell were those of changed lives, and people transformed and healed by the power of Jesus Christ. My experience with God, up to that point in my life, offered very little to help others. I needed something more. I needed change in my life if I desired to go to another level…or to ride a horse.

A man can walk on a higher level or more specifically, in the power and glory of God when he learns to do five simple things:

1. To ride a horse, one must grab the horn of the saddle and pull himself up.

My first exposure to real revival initially left me unimpressed and cautiously critical. Reports were being spread that a new move of God was taking place in Pensacola, Florida, which appeared to be much like the Azusa Street Revival in the early 1900s. From around the world, people began attending these services that began on Father's Day in 1995. As I sat on the back pew in the balcony, the experience I had raised more questions than I had answers for. I told my church leadership team I had brought with me that I had been in Pentecost all my life, but I had never seen or heard anything like that before. I suggested we take the experience with a grain of salt and see what came of it. We left the next morning and headed back to Texas. I don't know when or where it was along the six hundred mile trip, but by the time we got back to Corrigan, a raging fire burned inside all of us.

Is there a desire stirring inside you that involves things you want to see God do in your life? If so, the question you have is no different from mine: "Lord, is this desire from you or is it my overactive imagination?"

I am convinced a person or congregation must have their own revelation. One cannot copy or mimic a move of God somewhere else or something seen, being done in others. When God births something new inside a man, the DNA of that experience, with the anointing or the gifting which brought him into this new place, will be manifest and evident in what comes out of him. When God touched me with the fire of His presence I first experienced at Pensacola, it continued to manifest in my life and in the lives of the others that were with me.

I had to get out of my comfort zone, get my ideas out of my head, and let God fill me with new ones. People said, "You don't have to go to Pensacola to find God," which is true. But how many people leave town for a vacation when there is a motel in your own city? When was the last time people you knew went out of their way to eat at a particular restaurant when there was a kitchen in their own homes? Men are willing to travel great distances to shop at a popular sporting goods store when the local department store has a complete sporting goods section. Likewise, Abraham would not be blessed until he left his own country and followed God. I have no problem when God calls and gives instructions to make a journey.

Let me go back to my initial thought about revival services in Pensacola where I, and those with me, received a powerful impartation. We travelled home and enjoyed this blessing until our blessing ran out, and we felt the need to return for another filling. It was after one of these many trips that God spoke to my heart and said, "You can't keep drinking from someone else's well." With the same voice, I heard Him promise me He would "send revival to my church," but I had to first "dig my own well." The promise came clearly to me, one I will never forget. The promise was, if I would do here what they did there, I would see here what they were seeing there.

It was at this point in my life I realized I had to have my own experience with God in regard to what He wanted to do in my life and ministry. I find it is much easier to live off someone else's experience and sacrifice, much like drinking from a well that someone else dug. To write the new chapters in my life, it would involve my personal sacrifice and preparation. I had to grab hold of this new thing and embrace it for myself. I had to discover this experience, which was bigger than me, and pull myself up to it. To ride a horse, there is only one way you can get on, and that is to grab hold of the horn of the saddle and pull yourself up.

The word *grab* in the Merriam-Webster dictionary means to "seize." It is time to seize an opportunity greater than what you have and never let go. The thing you will be grabbing is something that may be out of your character or comfort zone, but it will bring results and satisfaction like nothing else you have ever tried.

You may have to adapt to a new way of praying and seeking God. This intensity of hunger for His presence will lead to a new way of worship that will require more of your time. Sacrifice and change will come easy when your effort brings satisfaction and the results you have been longing for into your life.

2. To ride a horse, one must be able to stretch.

When His presence comes, it is much like a newborn baby that demands a lot of time and attention. When our eighty-eight week revival began in October 2004, everyone in our church had to put their schedules on hold. In order to experience all that we did, people literally gave up their lives to accommodate His presence. Because we are a small church, we did not have the luxury of hiring people to do the various jobs and everyone had to do things they would not normally prefer to do.

A new baby is known for being messy and demanding a lot of time. When spiritual activity increases, more people are brought into the Kingdom, which puts added stress on the other family members. Babies require a tremendous amount of patience and tender care. We must accept these new family members with all the mess that comes with them.

Once a man I met mentioned to me that he was aware of the extended services going on and the many reports of people being saved and healed. He said, "I have never attended the services, but I am just standing back and waiting to see if this is really a move of God." A feeling of agitation came over me as to why some people could not see this was truly a move of God. I realized many people judged the manifestations and the authenticity of the miracles to determine whether this was a true move of God.

When I attended other revivals, I wondered, "How does the move of God affect the members of the church?" I learned the most accurate indicator of a move of God is to watch the people who were serving. During revival I observed people. Even though some were parents who had children in school and worked full-time jobs, others were teenagers who skipped their dating years, but they all did so to be in His presence and serve others.

I used the term "outer perimeter" people to describe the members of my church who served in intercessory prayer, childcare, music, ministry teams, parking, security, cooking, sound, cleaning and many other areas so that crowds could come in and be blessed. Only living for a higher purpose would cause these gracious people to cheerfully give up their own seats, money, time, and reputation to serve others. Members had to stretch physically, spiritually, and financially to be a part of what God was doing. No one wanted to be left out, even though to serve on this level required arriving early and staying late, five services a week.

This was a very intense time of serving God, and some people did burn out. I would not trade anything in the world for this wonderful experience. It could only be His presence that could challenge us to serve faithfully and to keep that rigorous pace. The strength and commitment the members had in serving Him could only be explained as being supernatural in origin. No pastor can force this type of commitment out of a person—only a love of God can draw this type service from people. People who eventually began to be called out from that environment to serve in ministry in other places would carry a great anointing on their lives because so much time was spent in His presence.

To stretch could mean you lose your prejudice of other denominations, cultures, and styles of worship. I never knew there were so many different ways of worshipping God until I saw men of all colors and backgrounds come under one roof to seek Him. I remember the night a Baptist woman "kidnapped" her Presbyterian neighbor and brought her to an Assembly of God church, where she sat next to a Church of Christ woman and received her healing.

To stretch involves accepting all kinds of people from every walk of life without discrimination. Every Thursday evening, a sheriff from a neighboring county would allow the inmates in his correctional facility an opportunity to attend revival services. Naturally these men would jump at the chance to get out of their cell for an evening. These inmates were always perfect gentlemen and never presented a problem. On one particular night as the altar call was given, every one of the inmates went forward for salvation. It just so happened that a local city judge also attended, and neither the inmates nor the judge knew who the others were. The county inmates and the city judge all came forward, standing shoulder to shoulder, and prayed the sinner's prayer together.

Anytime you stretch, it allows for growth, personally and spiritually.

3. To ride a horse, one will have to know how to keep their balance.

You have to understand something about experiencing greater things from God. Once He touches you, some of His very own people may begin to distrust and resent you or become jealous of you. God is not going to exempt you from this, but He will give you the grace to deal with it. A lack of approval or acceptance never feels very good. Those feelings are especially difficult when they come from the ones who we are told are on the same team as ourselves.

I heard a wise pastor say once, "Pastors can be territorial and critical. If they see God doing something in another church that He is not doing in their own, they think it must not be God. Once convinced something is not from God, the pastors will not support what God is doing for fear their own people will be attracted to it."

I have learned to refuse to get into a spirit of competition with others. When something good begins to happen in another person's life and ministry, I have learned to celebrate it and commend them for the breakthrough. I doubt God would bless me with something that I criticized other pastors for, in their success.

One of my dearest friends is Lonnie Vallance who pastors a small church in the neighboring town of Groveton, not far from Corrigan. He is one of the most Kingdom minded pastors that I have ever met. During our extended revival, not only was he and his wife two of the most faithful attendees, but he would go home and publicize our services on his church marquis. The two towns are only eighteen miles apart and have a reputation across our state as having one of the longest running, fiercest football rivalries in Texas. When the Lord began to stretch Lonnie, it was for the purpose of blessing him. Rather than feel threatened by what God was doing in my church, he embraced it. Even though Groveton is a town smaller than Corrigan, Lonnie is experiencing wonderful blessings and is enjoying favor with other ministers in his own community.

You may not be a pastor, but you have probably experienced the same frustration when God touches your life—not everyone is going to understand you or like what God is doing. Some people will like you better when you are struggling, discouraged, and ready to quit. Please keep in mind how they feel and that once, you too struggled and were where they are. When God touches your life, be careful not to appear arrogant and prideful and always remember where you came from.

Let's recall the story in the book of 1 Kings 3, where two harlots were brought before King Solomon after the death of one of their infants. Both women had babies, but one of the mothers had rolled over and unknowingly smothered her infant as they slept. During the night the mother awoke and saw what had happened and exchanged her lifeless baby for the other mother's live one. The next morning, you can imagine the chaos when both women claimed the living baby. No one could figure out how to determine the real mother of the live baby so they brought the two women before King Solomon to make the decision. Solomon simply told them to bring him a sword and he would settle this quickly. Solomon informed both of the women they could each have a half of the living baby. The real mother, being terrified, screamed to let the other woman have the baby so her child would live, and in so doing, exposed the heart of the real mother. The mother of the dead infant had nothing to lose. Simply said, if someone cannot have their baby, it doesn't bother them for you to be without yours either.

If someone cannot be happy in their life and ministry, it doesn't bother them for you to be unhappy in yours. You have to learn to keep your balance because there will always be someone who wants to knock you off your horse. You may be ridiculed and lose friends on one level, but God will send you new friends on another.

4. To ride a horse, one must learn to trust the horse.

I will be the first to admit I have a healthy respect for horses. Several years ago, my brother-in-law was killed in a horse-related accident, which left my sister alone with four boys to raise. While on a trailride, one of my daughters fell off a horse and broke her arm. In the town where I live, many children have been kicked or severely injured by horses. When I am around horses, I have learned to be very careful because beautiful animals can still be dangerous.

I have a friend in the Texas hill country who is a real cowboy. He makes his living by training horses and leading trail rides. He gave me a standing offer that anytime I am in the area, he would take me riding. A few years ago, my wife and two of our daughters were near his ranch so we decided to visit him and ride horses. Knowing that I am an inexperienced horseman, my friend had the novel idea of putting his five-year-old granddaughter on a horse in front of me. There is nothing as humbling for an inexperienced grown man than to ride behind a young child that knows how to handle a horse.

As we were riding along the trail, we covered every type of terrain known to man. We went up hills, down into ravines, through creeks, travelled switchbacks, crossed through barbed wire fences, and walked along steep inclines. I found myself constantly attempting to steer the horse by pulling on the reins. When I noticed the horse seemed to be getting a little nervous and agitated, I grasped the reins a little tighter.

How could my friend's young granddaughter seem to make riding a horse appear so natural and the horse to be relaxed while my horse appeared jittery? I constantly watched to make sure my horse would not lose its footing while walking down a narrow path on a steep incline. As

I looked down, I noticed there were ruts carved into the rocky trail, and it became evident that these horses had been down this path many times before. All of a sudden, I realized the horses knew exactly where they were going and what they were to do. I had a choice—I could keep pulling on the reins, making my horse nervous and risk being thrown, or I could loosen up on the reins and trust the horse. Reluctantly I loosened the reins and the horse immediately appeared at ease. The horse just wanted to be trusted.

Often we do not trust God and what He is doing in our lives. We feel we must keep our hands tightly gripped on the reins as we are unsure of the path He is leading us down. Remember that you are not the first person He has taken down the path which you are on. He only wants you to completely trust Him.

5. If one's backside is sore, one is not using his knees enough.

Back at the corral, when our trail ride came to an end, my friend came directly to me and asked a very interesting question. He chuckled as he asked me, "Preacher, is your backside sore?" Though I am not much of a horseman, I had quickly realized during the ride that if I just sat on the horse, it was going to be a long and bumpy ride. While riding, the natural motion of the horse will cause one to be rubbed on their backside, giving them blisters. Being saddle sore is never a very good feeling.

When it comes to riding the horse or walking in this greater dimension, we must do something with this entrustment. Jesus gave the disciples what is known as the Great Commission. He expects the same from us.

And he said unto them, Go ye into all the world, and preach the gospel to every creature. He that believeth and is baptized shall be saved; but he that believeth not shall be damned. And these signs shall follow them that believe; In my name shall they cast out devils; they shall speak with new tongues; They shall take up serpents; and if they drink any deadly thing, it shall not hurt them; they shall lay hands on the sick, and they shall recover. So then after the Lord had spoken unto them, he was received up into heaven, and sat on the right hand of God. And they went forth, and preached every where, the Lord working with them, and confirming the word with signs following. Amen (Mark 16:15-20).

We cannot just sit and admire a gift and think, "This is wonderful." We are expected to use this gift as we walk this command out and not let it become just another spiritual experience. I believe the greatest days of the Church are ahead if we will take this message and run with it. The experience of riding a horse is the smoothest and most exhilarating when a horse is running in full stride. If you don't use your knees, it won't be long until you are either very sore, presenting a temptation for you to get off the horse, or you will learn to ride on this new level.

He giveth power to the faint; and to them that have no might he increaseth strength. Even the youths shall faint and be weary, and the young men shall utterly fall: But they that wait upon the LORD shall renew their strength; they shall mount up with wings as eagles; they shall run, and not be weary; and they shall walk, and not faint (Isaiah 40:29-31).

I thank God for strength which comes when we wait on the Lord. However, I sense the Lord is calling us into a season when He wants us to "ride the horses." Jeremiah tells us His horses are swifter than eagles (Jeremiah 4:13).

Are you tired of walking in circles with your life? Are you frustrated when good things happen to other Christians and not to you? Are you wondering why some Christians seem to be operating in an effective ministry and you find yourself wishing it was available to you? The good news is you don't have to stay where you are. Grab the horns of the saddle and pull yourself to a new level in the Lord. He is no respecter of persons and will withhold no good thing from you.

Remember, if you are willing to learn to ride a horse, He will give you one.

Chapter Four

Don't Miss Your Visitation

What will ye do in the day of visitation? (Isaiah 10:3)

The Lord promised in His Word there would be a last day revival. This revival must begin somewhere, in someone, and at sometime. If you truly believe revival is coming, your preparations should have already begun. Every move of God has its identifying elements, and it has not yet been revealed how this revival will feel when things begin to shift. No one knows who the key people will be, the style of music that will accompany it, or what the unique manifestations will be. You must make up your mind whether or not you will embrace it before it ever begins. You may not have the luxury of being able to study it long and hard. There may not be time to try to figure it out or test it. Your only choice to make is will you go after it? That decision must already be made in your heart, and you must have all the issues settled. And when it begins, you must never look back.

Solomon presented an interesting story of a man, after a long journey, who returned home late one night…

I sleep, but my heart waketh: it is the voice of my beloved that knocketh, saying, Open to me, my love, my dove, my undefiled: for my head is filled with dew, and my locks with the drops of the night. I have put off my coat; how shall I put it on? I have washed my feet; how shall I defile them? My beloved put in his hand by the hole of the door, and my bowels were moved for him. I rose up to open to my beloved; and my hands dripped with myrrh, and my fingers with sweet smelling myrrh, upon the handles of the lock. I opened to my beloved; but my beloved had withdrawn himself, and was gone: my soul failed when he spake: I sought him, but I could not find him; I called him, but he gave me no answer (Song of Solomon 5:2-6).

This husband travelled through the night just to be with the wife he loved and had missed. Before he arrived home, he spruced himself up with her favorite cologne and began to knock on the door. He lifted his hand and gave a couple of swift raps, which woke his wife from her deep sleep. He called out to her through the door that he was home, but before she jumped out of the bed to welcome him, she had to do some thinking. She realized it was the one she loved so dearly, but he didn't understand that she was already undressed and tucked into her warm, comfortable bed. She thought if she got up, she would have to get dressed and go back through the trouble of washing her feet a second time and to get undressed again just to get some sleep. She lay there pondering what she should do. A few minutes later, she fully awoke and thought to herself, *What was I thinking? My husband was outside the door and I should have let him in.*

As she rushed to the door, she could smell the fragrance where his hands had just handled the latch on the other side of the door. Unlocking the door, she swung it open, but her husband had already withdrawn himself. Because of her delay, he made the decision to return in the morning. While he had waited for her to arise from the bed and let him in, she laid comfortably on the other side of the door, wondering why he came at a time when she was cozy and warm. Once she opened the door and saw that he was not there, she looked into the alley and called his name, but he did not answer her. She ran after him and could not find him.

If you are not prepared and have it settled in your mind, you may miss the opportunity that could change your life. God seldom shows up at a time that is convenient. Because this visitation could be life-changing, you do not want to miss the very thing you have prepared for and waited for so long.

Moses too found out that God does not always show up at a convenient time. When the opportunity arises, you will always have a lot to gain...or a lot to lose.

Now Moses kept the flock of Jethro his father-in-law, the priest of Midian: and he led the flock to the backside of the desert, and came to the mountain of God, even to Horeb. And the angel of the LORD appeared unto him in a flame of fire out of the midst of a bush: and he looked, and, behold, the bush burned with fire, and the bush was not consumed. And Moses said, I will now turn aside, and see this great sight, why the bush is not burnt. And when the LORD saw that he turned aside to see, God called unto him out of the midst of the bush (Exodus 3:1-4).

Until this moment in the life of Moses, he was not a mighty man, not a miracle worker, nor the great deliverer of the children of Israel from Egyptian bondage. Up to this time, all that could be said about him was that he had a very interesting past. Having lived as the adopted son of Pharaoh's daughter, he had to run from the law after killing a man and hid out in the Arabian desert.

Moses took the only job he could find, one of watching the sheep for his father-in-law, Jethro. On a very uneventful day, looking up on a mountain, he observed a most unusual sight. He saw a bush that appeared to be on fire but never burned up. He was faced with a very difficult decision: should he take the sheep back to the sheepfold and return the next day to investigate this strange happening? Should he investigate the burning bush at that moment, hoping that a thief wouldn't steal the sheep or predators devour them as he left them unattended? If there was nothing to that unusual sight and he lost the sheep, Jethro would never forgive him, and the news of his careless behavior would make it impossible for him to acquire another job.

All the options seemed a good reason to remain with the sheep, but then he began to think, *What if there was something to the burning bush that would change my life?* It was this thought that convinced him to live life with no regrets, and he left the sheep alone and unattended.

Anytime it appears God is calling but you heard wrong, you have a lot to lose. If the voice actually is Him, and you turn to listen, it will be life-changing. God began to speak to Moses only after he turned aside to see. When he met with God, he received a mandate that not only changed the course of his life but also the history of the world. Many people will miss their moment of opportunity because they refuse to turn aside from their busy schedules for fear of failure or fear of man.

One of the first times in my life that I clearly heard the Lord speak to me was in May 1996. You never really know whether the voice is actually the Lord speaking or just an overactive imagination until you respond to what you have heard. I was mowing the church lawn one Saturday afternoon when I heard the voice I assumed to be the Lord. This voice clearly said three very simple words, "Go to Pensacola." I knew the voice meant the Brownsville Revival, as I had begun hearing people talk about the powerful services happening there. This was a very foreign thing for me to do because I was taught at an early age you don't have to go find God because He is everywhere. Desperation and curiosity demanded I do something I had never done before, and I walked right into His presence and my life was changed forever.

Twelve years later, in May 2008, I again heard the voice I assumed to be the Lord, telling me to take a trip to Lakeland, Florida. Healing services were being conducted by an evangelist at Ignite Church. The revival itself was certainly an event of controversy; and people were flocking to Lakeland from around the world, hoping the things they had been seeing and hearing were true. Although nightly healing services were being aired on an international Christian television channel, I wanted to investigate for myself, so I invited three other ministers and a deacon from my church to travel with me so we could see for ourselves.

The trip from Lakeland to Corrigan is about a twenty hour drive. On the way home, I contacted good friends, who have a retreat center in Church Point, Louisiana, and asked if five weary travelers could stay in their rooms. In exchange for a place to stay, I offered to share a word from the Lord and the Lakeland testimonies with any of their friends they could gather on the spur of the moment. No one knew that word of this meeting would spread rapidly across Louisiana and ultimately change two families in particular, as well as a neighboring community.

I want to share with you two different testimonies of women who had their lives changed when they dropped what they were doing and "turned aside to see."

The following is a testimony from Manon DeLoach who lives in Ville Platte, Louisiana, which is about an hour drive from Church Point. This testimony revolves around her then eighteen-year-old daughter named Gabrielle, who had been in a tragic car accident and had spent forty-two days in the hospital.

Gabrielle and I had been watching the Lakeland Revival on God TV for weeks. The presence of God was so strong in the room each night; and we knew if we could get there, God would meet us. Gabby had just started walking and really wasn't strong enough from weeks in the hospital and being in bed. She would get tired so fast, and she really needed a miracle, but we knew there was no way she could travel to Lakeland. A lady in our church has a sister from Church Point who called her and told her that a few pastors were on their way back from the revival and would have a healing and impartation service. We knew we somehow had to get to the service, but it was already 4:30 in the afternoon when she called and the service started at 6 pm. I called my husband and he told us to go. We met a few other people and jumped in our cars and we literally had no idea where we were going. I called my sister in Shreveport and told her we were going to an impartation service in Church Point and to call another friend, Rebecca LaFleur. She gave me the few directions she had, and we got there just in time. God did show up and healed Gabby's bladder—she felt it move on the inside. She went from severe leakage to absolutely none and then God healed her leg. I remember her knees being uneven when she walked and she had a severe limp. After her healing, her knees were even and she did not limp anymore!

I wonder what would have happened if Manon and Gabrielle had not been ready to go to the revival service at a moment's notice. Their lives were changed when they "turned aside to see." The story gets even better because of Rebecca LaFleur from Mamou, Louisiana, who Manon mentioned. Here is Rebecca's testimony.

After I got off work, I went to visit my sister. Leaving her house to pick up my grandbabies for the evening, my phone rang. It was a friend from Bossier City, Louisiana, who told me I had to get to Church Point to hear some pastors from Texas who have been to the Lakeland Revival in Florida. I had to make a quick decision about my grandchildren and made other arrangements for them so I could attend this meeting. Without knowing where I was going, I headed to Church Point to look for a barn in the middle of a field. The first place I saw, I stopped after seeing all the cars at a barn thinking I had found it, but it turned out to be a cockfight. The man I spoke to tried to get me to stay but I told him it wasn't the revival I was looking for. I finally arrived and the atmosphere in the place was electrified. I saw a young girl Gabrielle, whom I knew had been in a bad accident, and she was instantly healed. The rest of the night I lay on the floor under the Glory. Each time I tried to get up, one of the pastors passed near me and simply laid their hands on me and under the Glory I stayed. It was after midnight before I was able to speak to Pastor Phil for a few minutes to just say thank you for bringing the Glory to our area. On Sunday morning before I left for church, he called and said, "The Lord told me revival was coming to Mamou" and that "the Glory would fall in our church services." And fell it did and remains to this day to the Glory of God. I have witnessed so many miracles and different things that God has done in the City of Mamou as well as in my own family. Pastor Phil said that one day, he will write a book on the Mamou Revival and each of his trips here could make a different chapter.

Your defining moment could pass you by if you are not ready to spring into action. You only have one life, and you live it by your choices. Please don't miss your opportunity. You have to know what you are going to do in order to seize your opportunity, or you will let it pass you by before the moment ever arrives. In my mind, I always rehearse what I will do when the opportunity that I am preparing for presents itself. When that moment comes, I will not let it pass me by.

And Jesus saw them toiling in rowing; for the wind was contrary unto them: and about the fourth watch of the night he cometh unto them, walking upon the sea, and would have passed by them (Mark 6:48).

To run with your second wind, you must know what it is you are looking for, recognize it when it comes, and not let the moment pass you by.

Chapter Five

Position Yourself

And ye shall seek me, and find me, when ye shall search for me with all your heart (Jeremiah 29:13).

My parents had five children and I was the only boy. Now I am a father of four daughters with no sons. It can be said that much of my life has revolved around girls. As my four daughters became teenagers, I realized that what teenage girls enjoy and what a dad enjoys are two totally different things.

An older gentleman recently gave his heart to the Lord and began attending church with his family. Through my many visits with him and our growing friendship, I began to develop an interest in deer hunting. I will never forget making a visit to his home on a day he was sighting in his rifle, and he offered me the opportunity to shoot it. Once I fired the first shot, I felt the energy of the rifle along with the smell of the gunpowder, and I was hooked.

I visited my friend often, and he would tell me his deer stories and everything else he knew about hunting. I never tired of his stories, and each time I visited him, I would ask him to tell me the stories again. I have since become an avid hunter and spend as much time in the woods as my wife and the Lord will allow. My wife and daughters never seemed to enjoy hunting, but I now have fine sons-in-law who enjoy it and probably are much better at it than myself.

When I first began to develop my hunting skills, I would get frustrated because I never could seem to get a glimpse of a white-tail deer. I could always find tracks where deer had been, but I always failed to find tracks where they were. It was then that I had the revelation I had to change my tactics. I had to stop looking where I thought they were and start looking ahead to figure out where I thought they may be going.

I began to ask deer hunters every question I could think of and read every book I could find on the subject. I realized that I must get inside the head of a deer to discover what it might be looking for. I soon understood that a doe will be looking for something different than a buck, and I learned everything changed when the seasons changed. What a deer will feed on is different in the spring than in the fall. Deer react differently under a full moon compared to a new moon. Deer exhibit other patterns when there is an approaching weather system, and a buck throws all common sense to the wind when he goes into the rut. When a buck is in the rut (male deer reproductive cycle), he rarely eats and may travel several miles in a day while chasing a doe. When the acorns begin to fall to the ground, you will always find the deer close by.

For me, I discovered I could find God the same way I discovered how to find deer. You must figure out what a deer, or God, may be looking for. Studying tracks where deer have been will give insight as to what attracted them to that place or where they may be going. This could be the very information you need to know in order to position yourself to find them, or most importantly, Him. Seldom will a hunter just stumble upon a deer, especially a trophy buck.

A hunter must study the habits of deer. He must determine the direction of the wind, observe the terrain, discover the food sources, chart their watering holes and bedding areas, and decide what a deer is looking for under the varying conditions. He must then make a decision for his plan of action. Once the plan is made, it is just a matter of getting to the predetermined spot before the deer does. When a hunter knows what a deer is looking for and gets positioned, he will most likely have a sighting of this beautiful animal.

The best place to begin looking for deer is on their well established travel routes. Even in the forest, a good outdoorsman will always be able to pick up these paths that animals follow. Having all of this information may work for seeing a deer; but the question we are asking is, "Will this work in finding God?"

And Jesus entered and passed through Jericho. And, behold, there was a man named Zacchaeus, which was the chief among the publicans, and he was rich. And he sought to see Jesus who he was; and could not for the press, because he was little of stature. And he ran before, and climbed up into a sycamore tree to see him: for he was to pass that way. And when Jesus came to the place, he looked up, and saw him, and said unto him, Zacchaeus, make haste, and come down; for to day I must abide at thy house. And he made haste, and came down, and received him joyfully (Luke 19:1-6).

Zacchaeus, being a tax collector, I am sure was never invited to the social gatherings of the Jews or even the temple socials thrown by the Pharisees. Because he was small of stature, he could never see over the heads of those in the crowd ahead of him when Jesus was near.

Zacchaeus was frustrated because what he had been doing was not getting him anywhere near Jesus. He always saw where Jesus had been but never could actually see Him. In order to see Jesus, he knew he had to try and devise a plan. Because he was a tax collector, people naturally avoided him. Necessity demanded he study people's habits in order to find them to collect the taxes they owed, so his occupational skills came into play. To make his collections, he learned the daily travel pattern people would take and waited for them to come down the road. These skills gave him hope that he could actually see Jesus.

Zacchaeus had observed that Jesus often travelled a certain path each time He entered Jericho. He had knowledge of a sycamore tree with a very large limb that extended over the middle of the road. He may have seen children climbing it each time he passed. His plan was to break away from the crowd where Jesus was and get positioned out on the limb extending over the road where he thought Jesus might be going. It was a long shot but was the only possible way he could think of that might get him a glimpse of Jesus. If Zacchaeus were wrong, he would certainly look like a fool; but if he were right, the glimpse would be one that could possibly change his life. He pondered the possibilities and decided his plan might actually work.

It wasn't long before the noise of an excited mob of people began to be heard in the distance. Moments later, the crowd began to approach the sycamore tree where Zacchaeus had positioned himself. His heart began to race. No doubt, Zacchaeus got dizzy and almost fell out of the tree. What would Jesus say when He saw him? Would the crowd laugh at his plan?

As Jesus drew close, He looked up in the tree and saw this little man staring down at Him. Jesus told Zacchaeus to get down as quickly as he could because He wanted to visit with him in his home. During their visit together, it didn't take Zacchaeus long to repent, and he willingly confessed his sins and made full restoration to all those he had wronged.

Jesus had a wonderful reputation around Jericho. There is another story of a man who saw where Jesus had been and figured out where He was going. He too positioned himself for what he hoped would be nothing less than miraculous.

And they came to Jericho: and as he went out of Jericho with his disciples and a great number of people, blind Bartimaeus, the son of Timaeus, sat by the highway side begging. And when he heard that it was Jesus of Nazareth, he began to cry out, and say, Jesus, thou Son of David, have mercy on me. And many charged him that he should hold his peace: but he cried the more a great deal, Thou son of David, have mercy on me. And Jesus stood still, and commanded him to be called. And they call the blind man, saying unto him, Be of good comfort, rise; he calleth thee. And he, casting away his garment, rose, and came to Jesus. And Jesus answered and said unto him, What wilt thou that I should do unto thee? The blind man said unto him, Lord, that I might receive my sight. And Jesus said unto him, Go thy way; thy faith hath made thee whole. And immediately he received his sight, and followed Jesus in the way (Mark 10:46-52).

Notice that at first, "Jesus and His disciples came to Jericho" and then it says, "He went out of Jericho with His disciples and a great number of people." Blind Bartimaeus missed his opportunity when Jesus entered, but he was determined that if Jesus was going to leave by the same route He came in, he must devise a plan and be prepared to spring into action if the moment presented itself.

As Jesus approached, blind Bartimaeus immediately cried out, capturing the attention of Jesus, even though everyone demanded he remain silent. Of all the blind men in the crowd, Bartimaeus was the only one mentioned who received a miracle. In order to receive a miracle, you may have to do what other people are either unwilling to do or do not have the knowledge to do.

We have now discovered that a well-devised plan worked for a known sinner and for a blind man. Our question is, "Will Jesus stop what He is doing for the desire of the righteous?" In our pursuit of Jesus, we need to remember a couple of things about Him.

The first thing to remember as you seek Him is that He wants to be found as much as you want to find Him. The second thing to remember is that His greatest desire is to be desired. He will always make His presence known when He is desired. Sometimes we do the things we do to command His attention. When you get Him to stop, you never know what you will receive. Keep in mind that you never know what will happen until you get out on a limb. Just ask Zacchaeus.

In July 2006, our church sent our worship leader to Buenos Aires, Argentina, for the annual Breakthrough Conference at Rey de Reyes Church where Claudio Freidzon was the pastor. Before she left, I gave her a sponge and told her to soak up everything she could and bring it home. At the close of one of the meetings, there were hundreds of people during the impartation service lined up for prayer when Pastor Claudio saw this young lady, who wore a sponge around her neck attached to her name badge. He pointed her out and inquired why she had the sponge. She told him that she just represented a thirsty pastor and a lot of other thirsty people back in her home church in Corrigan, Texas. Someone then told him that she attended a church that was experiencing revival. After he laid hands on her and prayed, he began to prophesy as well. Claudio Freidzon exclaimed, "It's coming; it's coming even greater than before." When she did what others had not done, she received a very special impartation that others did not get.

In a setting where a man is flowing in a gift, I have learned that those who press in are more likely to receive ministry than the individual who just sits back and waits for something to happen. It might sound spiritual to say, "If he is a man of God, he will come to where I am and lay hands on me or give me a word." In reality, if you need something from God, have a plan and be aggressive.

I have seen countless miracles people received because they were determined to be the one the man of God sees or has to stumble over. I was preaching with this thought in mind in a church near San Antonio. I mentioned, "You must position yourself for a miracle." In this particular service, with the exception of the pastor and his wife, absolutely no one was sitting on any of the front rows of the four different sections of pews. As I said, "Be the one so close that the man of God stumbles over you," a lady in her late thirties stood up, made her way forward, and sat directly in front of me. Her action opened the gate for a rush of people to come forward during the middle of my message until every first and second pew across the entire church was filled with people needing a breakthrough. People, filled with hope, brought the healing presence of Jesus, and many people were delivered and healed, including the young lady who first made her way to the front pew and sat before me.

I was preaching a revival in Andrews, Texas, and a neighboring pastor asked if I could come to his church in Monahans to have a Sunday afternoon healing service. In this service, again I mentioned the necessity of positioning yourself like Zacchaeus did in order to receive a miracle. A group from Andrews came to that service and then returned home to attend the evening revival service there. A young lady, who was studying to be a nurse, heard me make that statement and positioned herself for her miracle. As I was standing during worship, I felt an impression that before I preached, I should minister to someone who had a hip problem. When it came time for me to preach, I looked across the sanctuary filled with people and asked who was in need of a healing in their hip. The young lady had positioned herself and was on the first row in the chair closest to the center aisle. She was the one I would have had to stumble over to walk down the aisle in that service. The moment I spoke, she responded, and the Lord immediately healed her.

During our extended revival services in Corrigan, I observed an evangelist who flowed in the Spirit with a healing gift. I concluded that people tire quickly when the anointing is on them, and they may not make it all the way to the back of the church where some people are waiting. If someone needs a miracle or a word, he or she should get as close to the anointing as possible. That is what Bartimaeus did.

And ye shall seek me, and find me, when ye shall search for me with all your heart (Jeremiah 29:13).

What have you done to capture Jesus' attention? Do something out of the ordinary. Do what others are not willing to do or do not have the knowledge to do and see what happens. Position yourself for whatever it is you need from God. Don't let Him pass you by.

Chapter Six

Win the Heart of the Man of God

He that receiveth a prophet in the name of a prophet shall receive a prophet's reward; and he that receiveth a righteous man in the name of a righteous man shall receive a righteous man's reward (Matthew 10:41).

I prayed a very simple prayer once, hoping, but not really believing, that the Lord would take me seriously. He answered it and my life was changed. That prayer was this, "Lord, I am so tired of reading about someone else's stories, would You please give me some of my own?" Stories of other peoples' success in ministry caused me to get a holy desperation for His supernatural presence in my life.

I have a small tract of land where my wife and I live and enjoy spending a lot of time in the woods. My neighbor owns a large tract of land located directly behind my property. He uses his land to grow hay so there are very few trees, quite the contrast to my property that is filled with timber. When I began hunting, to observe their beauty and learn their habits, I often would go out in the evening right before dark and watch deer cross his field to eat at his corn feeder. I would hide in the bushes with my binoculars in hand to watch the deer congregate as the timed spinner on his feeder would spring into action and sling corn for them to eat. This was really quite time consuming, not to mention all the pain I endured as I got bit by mosquitoes, chiggers, and ticks.

I had an idea one day. I decided I would get my own feeder with a bag of deer corn and place it on my property. I placed my feeder about a hundred yards from my house, and I hoped to be able to see deer in my yard like my neighbor saw every day in his field. The most amazing thing happened. Just as in my neighbor's field, deer began to gather at my corn feeder. I could watch deer with ease while I sat on my back porch and sipped my coffee, which was much easier than what I had been doing. I discovered that when I did what someone else had been successfully doing, I began to see what they had already seen.

Because this worked, I also went to the area where I planned to hunt and planted wheat, oats, rye grass, and clover. Deer love to eat, and now they would have a never-ending food source. It was amazing the deer that I began to see when I put forth a little effort.

My greatest revelations on finding God came while I spent time in the woods watching deer. God is not going to show up just anywhere, but He will go where He is wanted. It was then I learned if I would become the person He was looking for, or if we became the church He couldn't resist, He would always come.

I want to share with you what I learned on how to attract the presence of God to my life and my church. It wasn't an easy task, but the reward of His presence was worth any effort I had put forth. Remember that God's greatest desire is to be desired. When He gets the impression you can't and won't live without Him, then He will show up.

There is a story in the Bible of a woman from Shunem who is a perfect example of becoming a person that the man of God cannot pass by. Look at the following passage concerning this determined woman and her husband, who desired a visit from the man of God.

> *And it fell on a day, that Elisha passed to Shunem, where was a great woman; and she constrained him to eat bread. And so it was, that as oft as he passed by, he turned in thither to eat bread. And she said unto her husband, Behold now, I perceive that this is an holy man of God, which passeth by us continually* (2 Kings 4:8-11).

In the little town of Shunem near Jezreel, we find a couple who observed Elisha the prophet walking in front of their home on a daily basis. They had a desire to do something for the man of God and devised a plan to get him to stop for lunch and some much needed rest. This couple from Shunem wanted to find a way to capture his attention and make him stop dead in his tracks.

Every man has a pattern he follows on a daily basis. Man was created in the image of God who is a God of patterns or cycles. God has His pattern for all of creation. He has a pattern for the seasons, the calendar, the days of the week, and the tides in the ocean. God even has a pattern for His house we call the tabernacle. When you realize that man and God are both very predictable, you can devise a plan on how to capture their attention.

The Shunammite woman knew two things that were certain. The first thing she knew was that Elisha always passed a certain way, at a certain time of day, everyday. The second thing she knew was that all men get hungry. Her plan had to be executed perfectly because there would never be a second chance to make a good first impression. She decided that she would bake Elisha a loaf of fresh bread and have her baking timed to bring the bread out of the oven at exactly the time he passed in front of her home. This determined woman probably made sure the window was open, hoping the aroma of the fresh baked bread would be more than he could resist.

Now this loaf of bread she had prepared to offer was not like one of our ordinary loaves of bread. This was not something she had picked up at the local supermarket but rather something that she had produced with her own hands. She had tilled the ground, planted the seed, and did all the things that it takes to make a garden grow. Planting the garden also required a lot of care until the wheat came into maturity and was harvested. Once harvested, there were many steps involved in the preparation before the wheat actually became a loaf of bread and was placed on the table. Anytime a woman baked a loaf of fresh bread, it was a labor of love.

How could a hungry man resist an opportunity to visit a home that gave him the feeling he was welcomed? The scripture never says that Elisha had a wife to cook for him or a family to give him company. This invitation to sit at a table and feel welcomed had to be an offer for Elisha that he could not refuse. Because he felt very welcomed while he sat at their table, he actually began to hope each time he passed by that fresh bread would be baked and ready to be served.

After many such occasions of sitting at their table and enjoying the company, he really began to feel right at home. It was then the

Shunammite woman realized there is one more thing that men desire. It was obvious after several visits that like most other men do after a good meal, Elish began to yawn, suggesting that a nap would be quite nice. After one such visit when Elisha left their home, the woman suggested to her husband that it would be a kind gesture to prepare a guest room designed to allow Elisha a chance to rest after eating one of her meals.

Let us make a little chamber, I pray thee, on the wall; and let us set for
him there a bed, and a table, and a stool, and a candlestick: and it shall
be, when he cometh to us, that he shall turn in thither. And it fell on a
day, that he came thither, and he turned into the chamber, and lay there
(2 Kings 4:10-11).

Her idea might have appeared to be farfetched, but her husband seemed to think the plan just might work. There was a section of the house that was never used, so they prepared a little chamber, brought in a bed, a table, a stool, and a candlestick, and offered him a place to rest after eating. They knew they could get him for a visitation but could this be turned into a habitation? It didn't take long for them to have their answer as Elisha could not refuse their hospitality and a place to rest.

Could it be that through practical ways we could show the Lord how much we want His presence? It takes more than saying we want His presence or praying that He comes. We must be willing to prepare for Him a place to rest.

Could it be we could win the heart of God the way we would win the heart of a man? We were created in the image and likeness of God. Can a man use the ordinary, common act of cooking to entice God to a place and please Him?

Let me show you two examples of God being drawn to a place because of the smell of good cooking. In the Old Testament temple, God was always attracted to the smell of sacrifice. If God was pleased, His presence would come down and He would forgive the sins of the people. This smell from the burnt sacrifice that the priest offered would ascend up to heaven and please God. The Lord then gave instructions to the priests that they could eat the roasted meat which had been offered.

Barbecue is enjoyed all across the United States, but nowhere is it as popular as here in Texas. There is something special about that occasion when the pit is fired up and the coals are red hot. You quickly become the envy of all your neighbors, as the smell of sizzling fat and your secret blend of spices permeate the air. If you want to welcome a guest to your home, there is no better way than when you are grilling.

We can find another example of God being drawn to a place because of the aroma coming from the inner court of the tabernacle. On the first day of each week, the priests were commanded to bring a fresh loaf of bread, one from each tribe, and place it on the table of shewbread. The priest and the Lord met face to face there. Each week as a new loaf was placed on the table, the priests were allowed to take the bread from the previous week home to eat.

I believe God uses natural hunger, much like spiritual hunger, to draw us from the outer court to the inner court. Once inside the entry dividing the outer from the inner, priests were given a choice to step toward the golden candlestick, which represented the power and enlightenment of the Holy Spirit, or toward the table of shewbread. God knew the greatest desire in man was to eat so man should choose the table over the candlestick, or as we can understand it, choose a relationship with God before the power of God.

As I said before, God's greatest desire is to be desired. Too often we only come to Him when everything else has failed and nothing has gone right. Could God get frustrated with us for wanting Him only for the way He can make us feel or for the things He can do for us? When was the last time you knew someone who really wanted Him just because they desired Him?

I understand a few things about pastors because I am one. Pastors live their lives among people who often need something. Please understand me, pastors don't mind helping in any way possible, but there are some people who just refuse to listen. When a pastor gives them scriptural advice, they will not follow through with it. Yet they want him to rush over and fix their marriage, help with attitudes in the kids, pray with them, or just listen to their problems one more time. When pastors are called on by these people to help, they may grumble to their spouse but will eventually make their way, dragging their feet, not really wanting to go again. They will do what they have already done a dozen times before and do it with a smile.

On the other hand, call the pastor and tell him everything is lovely and that nothing is wrong; tell him you have a fresh peach cobbler coming out of the oven in just a few minutes and fresh coffee is brewing. To top it off, you hint that you have a fresh carton of vanilla ice cream to go with it. By the time he is off the phone, he is already running out the door, breaking the speed limit just to get to your home. He may drag his feet in response to your problem, but he will quickly arrive at your home to sit at your table. When you offer a man what he desires, he will never refuse your invitation.

Many years ago, a lady who attended our church came to my wife and I and told us that her husband had kicked her out of the house and refused to let her return home. I told her I knew of a way that would ensure she could go back home. The plan was she would bake her husband his favorite pie, which I discovered happened to be lemon. I told her, "Do not go to the store and buy the cheap frozen one." I said, "Bake him one but start it with his favorite homemade crust." I advised her to go out of her way to make it exactly the way he loved it. A week later I asked her, "Did you make your husband a fresh lemon pie, and were you able to go back home?" She said, "I was able to go home but I didn't bake him his favorite fresh lemon pie." She saw the stunned look on my face, chuckled, and added, "I baked him *two* of them."

It is amazing the things that will happen and the situations that could change if we would just find out what a man is thinking. We have discovered that it works for deer, it works for a man, and it will work for God. We have to understand, the Kingdom is practical. Become the person the Lord desires. Give Him your best service and be the one He cannot refuse. When a person or even a congregation becomes who or what He is looking for, you can always find His presence.

> *He that receiveth a prophet in the name of a prophet shall receive a prophet's reward; and he that receiveth a righteous man in the name of a righteous man shall receive a righteous man's reward* (Matthew 10:41).

Even though I feel I have a good understanding of the Bible, the above scripture always seemed to puzzle me. Once I learned this principle and decided to practice it, it began to produce wonderful blessings in my life. Every man or woman of God has something good they can do for others. When they feel they are respected or appreciated, it seems to bring out the anointing in them. The gift they have to share may be a word of faith, a gift of healing, or a word of knowledge.

When someone listens attentively to the minister as he speaks, it shows him he is heard and it may pull the anointing from him. On the other hand when someone watches the clock, clips their fingernails, or falls asleep while he speaks, it sends a message they are not interested. Personally I am drawn to and respond better to those who at least appear to be interested in the things I say. Are we not created in God's image? Does God not react the same way? Again, God's greatest desire is to be desired. When you desire Him, He will always respond.

Draw nigh to God, and he will draw nigh to you... (James 4:8).

On an occasion when I was requested to preach a funeral, my hair needed to be trimmed, so I called my hairdresser for an appointment. She told me she had been sick with a migraine headache for three days. She was about to finish her last customer, travel home, and go straight to bed. Though she was not feeling well, I pleaded with her to cut my hair. Finally she told me to get there as quickly as I could, and she would cut it for me. When she agreed to cut my hair, I was determined that I would pray a prayer of faith after she finished because of her generosity. I sat in the chair and waited for the moment when she finished so I could offer a quick prayer. I casually brought up the subject of her migraine, and she started shaking her head and said, "It's gone; it's gone!" She couldn't believe what had just happened. I cannot prove the headache going away that day had anything to do with me, but as she cut my hair, the migraine left before I could even pray.

I believe that in men and women of God, spiritual gifts are in operation. My thought had been, *she went out of her way for me; I need to do something nice in return.* The best thing I could think of to do for her was to believe for her miracle. Migraines can come and go, but in her case, her migraines would last for up to six weeks at a time, and she could not even stand someone to be in the same room with her. It's now fifteen years later, and she recently testified to me that she "has yet to have another migraine."

In 1 Corinthians 12, two specific operations mentioned are "gifts of healing" and "working of miracles." If there truly is such a thing as the "gifts" of the Spirit, then it seems reasonable to believe they were meant to be shared. How they are distributed or shared is left to the leading of the Spirit and the discretion of the man or woman who walks in that anointing.

For to one is given by the Spirit the word of wisdom; to another the word of knowledge by the same Spirit; To another faith by the same Spirit; to another the gifts of healing by the same Spirit; To another the working of miracles; to another prophecy; to another discerning of spirits; to another divers kinds of tongues; to another the interpretation of tongues: But all these worketh that one and the selfsame Spirit, dividing to every man severally as he will (I Corinthians 12:8-11).

Jesus suffered the scourging and shed His precious blood on the cross for our salvation and healing, which is available to every single person in the world simply by looking to Jesus. What is a gift of working of miracles? Are there miracles that can be received when a man or woman of God simply desires to release it? If you don't believe it, just look what happened as the story of the Shunammite continues.

He (Elisha) said to Gehazi his servant, Call this Shunammite. And when he had called her, she stood before him. And he said unto him, Say now unto her, Behold, thou hast been careful for us with all this care; what is to be done for thee? wouldest thou be spoken for to the king, or to the captain of the host? And she answered, I dwell among mine own people. And he said, What then is to be done for her? And Gehazi answered, Verily she hath no child, and her husband is old. And he said, Call her. And when he had called her, she stood in the door. And he said, About this season, according to the time of life, thou shalt embrace a son (2 Kings 4:12-16).

We have seen in this story the Shunammite woman's hospitality and her acts of kindness in preparing meals and providing a place of rest for the man of God. Elisha sees this as an act of kindness that cannot be overlooked or go unrewarded. Elisha thought that she had a favor to ask of him as the motive behind her generosity. Elisha was willing to speak to the king for her or the captain of the host, and she simply replied that, "She did well among her own people."

When was the last time you wanted God for just who He is and not what He can give you or how He can make you feel? The Shunammite woman was not expecting anything in return. This woman and her husband only wanted to be with him.

Elisha couldn't just say, "Thank you." He felt he needed to do something but couldn't think of what it could be. He called his servant Gehazi and asked if he knew of anything that could be done for them. Without much thinking, he replied, "There were no children in the house, no toys, and no playroom." It was obvious that something was missing and probably longed for by the couple, and Elisha chose to do something about it.

Elisha called the woman back into the room and told her, "By this time next year, you will hold a child in your arms." Notice he didn't pray, rebuke, or bind, he simply spoke. She and her husband were just looking for his company, and she ended up with a baby. The very thing she desired, the thing she thought she would never have because she was barren, came to her as the result of their pursuit for the man of God's presence. When you win the heart of the man of God, you may very well be the receiver of untold blessings.

Heaven is My throne, the earth is My footstool: Where is the house you will build for Me? And where is the place of My rest? (Isaiah 66:1 NKJV).

In the above passage, we find what God is looking for. If you provide the Lord with a place to rest, He will come. If you provide Him with a table, you may have your visitation. Provide Him with an inner chamber, and you will have yourself a habitation. Give Him what He is looking for, and you just might end up with your dream coming to pass.

Amazing things happen when you get the attention of the man of

God. I was preaching a healing service at a church in Mexia, Texas, and saw healing take place in a strange way. Now let me explain, the pastor there had the novel idea that people should be fed after every revival service. The pastor is from Louisiana so he brought his mother and one of her friends from New Orleans to cook some Cajun food to feed everyone at the close of the service.

The Cajun women were working feverishly to prepare gumbo, étouffée, rice, and all the trimmings for when the service was finished. I was standing in the front row with my hands lifted and trying to worship as the service began. The two cooks came in the sanctuary and sat about four rows behind me. When these women entered through the swinging doors that divided the fellowship hall from the sanctuary, I got a heavenly whiff of the Cajun food cooking. The delicious aroma floated up to the front pew and slapped me in my face so that I could barely concentrate on the service. When the aroma of the food traveled from my nose to my brain, the thought came to me, *The cook needs a healing between her shoulder blades.* I turned to identify which cook this was, and I made up my mind that she, before anyone else that night, would receive her healing.

The service progressed, and after I preached a message on divine healing, I opened the altars for a time of ministry. I told the people, "The Lord has shown me someone with a terrible pain between their shoulder blades and that she should come forward for a healing." I also said, "I think I could identify who the person is, but I want to give them a chance to respond." No one came forward so I glanced to where the woman had been sitting, but she was gone. While I had been praying, she had quietly gotten up and went to the fellowship hall to finish preparing the food. I sent someone to ask her if she had a pain between her shoulder blades, and she replied, "Yes, but how did you know?" The person asking her said, "The preacher said he knew it." She came out of the kitchen, down the aisle, and before I even prayed for her or laid hands on her, I asked her to test her shoulders and see if there was any pain. She reported there was "none at all"—it was completely gone!

Praise God for that simple healing. It was not cancer, neither was it life threatening, but if something brings pain or discomfort, it should be dealt with. I praised God for this miracle, though it appeared a minimal one. The pastor called the next morning and said, "You have no idea how big that miracle was last night." He went on to tell me she had severe kidney problems, and often they would not even function. When this woman received the miracle between her shoulder blades, it released a pinched nerve that was cutting off the electrical impulses to her kidneys and now they functioned properly. This miracle began to happen because something she was cooking hit a chord in my nostrils before I preached, all because I love good Cajun cooking.

Rather than criticize another person's success in ministry, why don't we learn from how they have done things to attract the blessing or the presence of the Lord in their life? If we do some of the things they have done, we might start seeing results similar to what they have seen.

Win the heart of the man of God and you win his gift. Win the heart of God, and you win His presence. To run with your second wind means you must get proactive, don't wait for Him to come to you, but rather find a way to get His attention. Remember what David discovered:

In thy presence is fulness of joy; at thy right hand there are pleasures for evermore (Psalms 16:11).

Chapter Seven

Let's All Go Up to the Mountain

Come ye, and let us go up to the mountain of the LORD (Isaiah 2:3).

God is looking for a resting place, though He is never weary. He will stop what He is doing in order to dwell with us. Isaiah 66:1 asks the question, "Where is the house that ye build unto me?" The Lord exclaimed in Exodus 25:8, "Let them make me a sanctuary; that I may dwell among them."

I wish I could tell you the place He is attracted to is on the well-travelled path and is easy to find, but that is not where you will find His house. It is often in a hard to reach place so as to keep away those who would not really treasure it. You will never just stumble onto it by chance, but you must seek it out to find it.

When David had sinned against God and the hand of the Lord came against him, his only hope for himself and Israel was to offer a sacrifice. Even though Araunah had offered David his threshing floor at no cost to him, David refused to offer a burnt offering at a place that did not cost him. Scholars tell us that this very place, where he paid full price for the barn, was the same place that he later set aside for the building of the first temple.

> *And the king said unto Araunah, Nay; but I will surely buy it of thee at a price: neither will I offer burnt offerings unto the LORD my God of that which doth cost me nothing. So David bought the threshingfloor and the oxen for fifty shekels of silver* (2 Samuel 24:24-25).

The place the Lord desires to meet with us may not be in a plush valley or a comfortable building. This place will be on a path that is difficult to reach and few will find. We see in Isaiah that the place where the Lord wanted His House to be built was on the top of a mountain.

And it shall come to pass in the last days, that the mountain of the LORD's house shall be established in the top of the mountains, and shall be exalted above the hills; and all nations shall flow unto it. And many people shall go and say, Come ye, and let us go up to the mountain of the LORD, to the house of the God of Jacob; and he will teach us of his ways, and we will walk in his paths. ...Go up to the mountain, and bring wood, and build the house; and I will take pleasure in it, and I will be glorified, saith the LORD (Isaiah 2:2-3 and Haggai 1:8).

God doesn't mind putting a challenge before you. Elijah put a challenge to the widow at Zarephath. God challenged a boy on a battlefield with a giant, and a man prayed in a den full of lions. David declared in 2 Kings 22:14, "in my trouble I have prepared for the house of the Lord."

A journey to the top of the mountain was only the beginning of the challenge. The people of God were not allowed to build with rubble or stone readily available at the top but were told to bring the materials to build the house with them. This project would not be easy and some would even consider quitting. Remember, for Moses to bring the people out of Egypt, it was not enough to just pack their bags and leave, but they were also faced with a hot burning desert to cross. God wants to give the Kingdom to those who will not be troubled with the cost. When you do not have an investment in your venture, there will not be much to lose if you give up. In the words of an old familiar saying, "Easy come, easy go."

You cannot simply gather up the rubble that doesn't work anymore and put together something from it that is meaningful. The effort that attracts God may or may not resemble anything you have ever been asked to do before. Too often it is tempting to pattern what you think the next wave of revival will look like after what you last saw. Remember, every wave of revival that you may have ever seen eventually ran its course, finished its season, and fulfilled its purpose.

We often attempt to memorialize a wonderful experience and want to remain on that mountain. Let me remind you that God is always moving. When Peter, James, and John were with Jesus upon the mountain the night He was transfigured, they asked Jesus if they could build three tabernacles, as if this was a place they intended to stay at or return to.

And after six days Jesus taketh Peter, James, and John his brother, and bringeth them up into an high mountain apart, And was transfigured before them: and his face did shine as the sun, and his raiment was white as the light. And, behold, there appeared unto them Moses and Elias talking with him. Then answered Peter, and said unto Jesus, Lord, it is good for us to be here: if thou wilt, let us make here three tabernacles; one for thee, and one for Moses, and one for Elias (Matthew 17:1-4).

I love the stories from the "Voice of Healing" revivals in the 1950s and 60s, but A.A. Allen, Jack Coe, and William Branham are not coming back. Many attempt to live on past memories, never looking to the future for God to raise up another person or do something new. If those days are not coming back, let's look ahead and see what is on the horizon. You may not like the music, the new effective methods of ministry, or even the personalities that God may be using. However, if you do not get on board, you may find yourself a bitter, critical Christian, living in the past.

The biggest obstacle to what God is about to do is the last thing He did. Some people just cannot get over yesterday. You usually find the biggest critics of any move of God are the ones who were on the cutting edge of the last thing He did.

We forget the move of God we cherish wasn't always without controversy. The manifestations were misunderstood, and often the integrity of its ministers may have been brought into question. Our lives were changed by it, so we focus on the positive and exhibit grace with the negative. If we are not careful, we will not allow the Holy Spirit to usher us into something fresh and new. If you are waiting for a perfect revival to be embraced and received by everyone, you will be disappointed. I have decided I will embrace the less than perfect move of

God until the perfect revival comes along. I like to think of it in the terminology that Solomon used:

A living dog is better than a dead lion (Ecclesiastes 9:4).

God's presence in a church is something every generation of believers has to decide if they want for themselves. If they do desire His presence, the price is never cheap nor the labor easy. Each person must work together in unison to see God's desire accomplished. King Saul never had a desire for the presence of God. It did not matter to him that after the ark had fallen into the hands of the Philistines, to ever make an attempt to bring it back to Jerusalem. After Saul's death, David desired to return the ark back to its rightful place, but he knew he could not do it alone. David consulted with the leaders of Israel on every level, and they were all in agreement it was the proper thing to do.

> *And David consulted with the captains of thousands and hundreds, and with every leader. And David said unto all the congregation of Israel, If it seem good unto you, and that it be of the LORD our God, let us send abroad unto our brethren every where, that are left in all the land of Israel, and with them also to the priests and Levites which are in their cities and suburbs, that they may gather themselves unto us: And let us bring again the ark of our God to us: for we enquired not at it in the days of Saul. And all the congregation said that they would do so: for the thing was right in the eyes of all the people. So David gathered all Israel together, from Shihor of Egypt even unto the entering of Hemath, to bring home the ark of God* (1 Chronicles 13: 1-5).

It is not a wise thing for a pastor or even a few people in the church to attempt to "force" His presence on others. People are often comfortable and do not want to be disturbed. Even though the presence brings blessings, along with it will come challenges that many are not prepared to embrace. His presence may not cause a church to grow. Often, sadly, when He shows up, many people will leave. A church, their pastor, and the leadership team must be in one accord. I believe that if the pastor, as the leader, doesn't want the presence, it probably is not going to be welcomed. When God moves, He will always begin with the pastor who is head of the local church. David was wise in making sure everyone was on the same page with him.

Nehemiah had a very hard time convincing people they should return back to God. When he received permission to rebuild the walls around Jerusalem, he soon found out it wasn't just the walls that had been broken down. People had also lost a desire for the presence of God.

> *Then contended I with the rulers and said, "Why is the house of God forsaken?* (Nehemiah 13:11)

When Haggai the prophet questioned people about rebuilding the Lord's House, he too met much opposition. When God's presence is not desired, things we are involved in never come to fruition. Haggai finally convinced the people to turn back to God and rebuild the temple, giving the Lord a home.

> *This people say, The time is not come, the time that the LORD's house should be built. Then came the word of the LORD by Haggai the prophet, saying, Is it time for you, O ye, to dwell in your cieled houses, and this house lie waste? Now therefore thus saith the LORD of hosts; Consider your ways. Ye have sown much, and bring in little; ye eat, but ye have not enough; ye drink, but ye are not filled with drink; ye clothe you, but there is none warm; and he that earneth wages earneth wages to put it into a bag with holes....Ye looked for much, and, lo it came to little; and when ye brought it home, I did blow upon it. Why? saith the LORD of hosts. Because of mine house that is waste, and ye run every man unto his own house* (Haggai 1:2-9).

When Haggai put the challenge before the people, God stirred up the politicians, the preachers, and the people. I can only imagine what would happen today if we could get everyone on board with what God wants to do.

> *Then spake Haggai the LORD'S messenger in the LORD'S message unto the people, saying, I am with you, saith the LORD. And the LORD stirred up the spirit of Zerubbabel the son of Shealtiel, governor of Judah, and the spirit of Joshua the son of Josedech, the high priest, and*

*the spirit of all the remnant of the people; and they came and did work
in the house of the LORD of hosts, their God* (Haggai 1:13-14).

In Corrigan, as the congregation and I pursued the presence, I discovered the Lord doesn't need to see a finished product to begin to
bless. He just wants to see you lift the shovel and begin clearing the
rubble. The moment Israel began to prepare the ground, blessings
started flowing. The blessing of the Lord could be traced to the exact
day, before a single stone was laid, the moment they made up their mind
to return to the Lord.

*And now, I pray you, consider from this day and upward, from before a
stone was laid upon a stone in the temple of the LORD: ...Consider
now from this day and upward, from the four and twentieth day of the
ninth month, even from the day that the foundation of the Lord's temple
was laid, consider it...from this day will I bless you* (Haggai 2:15, 18).

With the people rebuilding the temple, the Lord began making
promises.

*And I will overthrow the throne of kingdoms, and I will destroy the
strength of the kingdoms of the heathen; and I will overthrow the char-
iots, and those that ride in them; and the horses and their riders shall
come down, every one by the sword of his brother* (Haggai 2:22).

Now listen to this promise...and you know the rest of the story.

*The glory of this latter house shall be greater than of the former saith the
Lord of Hosts* (Haggai 2:9).

I often tell people that my dream is greater than my memory. Some
will never experience greater things in the Lord because their memory is
too good. Those "good ole days" of revivals past are not coming back.
Their memories and all they hold will not compare to what He desires
to do. God always saves His best for the last. If we prepare ourselves
and get in position for the next wave, we just might catch it. The next
thing God does is greater than the last thing He did. When your first
wind has run its course, catch your "second wind."

Chapter Eight

Living in the Promise but not the Presence

My presence shall go with thee, and I will give thee rest (Exodus 33:14).

The children of Israel were not in the wilderness long until the novelty of the journey had run its course. Until this point, the travels had been exciting. They had had their first taste of freedom in almost five hundred years from Egyptian captivity. After crossing the Red Sea, they had seen the armies of Pharaoh perish in the depths of the water. At Rephidim they drank water from a rock after Moses struck it. At Sinai they saw the mountain smoke and quake at the presence of the Lord as Moses received the Ten Commandments. Now what lay before them was a hot, burning desert, which was the only thing that separated them from their inheritance across the Jordan River. All appeared to be going well until the people began to complain. When the path got tough and people grew tired of the manna, they began to question the decisions Moses was making. Israel started looking back to the land of bondage, preferring it to the land flowing with milk and honey just ahead.

Once the people began looking back, God had to make a decision whether or not He would continue on the journey with the Israelites. God is true to His Word and character and will always keep His promises. He had described Israel as a "stiff necked" people because they were so busy looking back, they could not move forward. God knew if He did not withdraw Himself, in His anger He would destroy them.

And the Lord said unto Moses, Depart, and go up hence, thou and the people which thou hast brought up out of the land of Egypt, unto the land which I sware unto Abraham, to Isaac, and to Jacob, saying, Unto thy seed will I give it: And I will send an angel before thee; and I will drive out the Canaanite, the Amorite, and the Hittite, and the Perizzite, the Hivite, and the Jebusite: Unto a land flowing with milk and honey: for I will not go up in the midst of thee; for thou art a stiff-necked people: lest I consume thee in the way (Exodus 33:1–3).

God said He would keep the promise He made to Abraham, Isaac, and Jacob. They would receive the inheritance, which was a land flowing with milk and honey. He also said He would send an angel before them to drive out the inhabitants until the land belonged to them. All this sounded pretty good until He advised them that He would not be going with them.

How or why would a person or congregation go forward without the presence of God? The answer is simple: there are two different ways of thinking. God was thinking holiness and the people were thinking comfort and entertainment.

Good things can happen without the presence of God. I believe people can be saved, delivered, and healed even if God's presence is nowhere to be found. Ministries can grow large, churches can overflow, books can sell, and concerts can be packed, all because God sent an angel or "one who is anointed" to get the job done. He may even use one who is in a backslidden condition. God still honors His Word and the faith of individuals. The anointing a person carries, while flowing in a gift, is not the same as the presence of God being present in a place. The scriptures tell us "… For the gifts and calling of God are without repentance" (Romans 11:29). Never determine God's presence by what you see; apparent success in ministry can be deceiving. God can use any man or woman even if they have lost ground in their walk with Him.

Many will say to me in that day, Lord, Lord, have we not prophesied in thy name? and in thy name have cast out devils? and in thy name done many wonderful works? And then will I profess unto them, I never knew you: depart from me (Matthew 7:22–23).

God will let a person, a church, or a nation continue to their promise, yet without His presence. You can live in the promise, the provision, or protection and still not be living in the presence of God.

And Moses took the tabernacle, and pitched it without the camp, afar off from the camp, and called it the Tabernacle of the congregation. And it came to pass, that every one which sought the Lord went out unto the tabernacle of the congregation, which was without the camp (Exodus 33:7).

Often when I take trips to minister in other places, my wife is not able to go with me. Before I leave, I make sure the grass is mowed, the cupboards are full, and there is a full tank of gas in our car. However, if you were to ask my wife if the things I provide are the same as me being there, the answer would always be no.

God withdrew His presence and told Moses to place the tabernacle outside the camp. Anyone who wanted to seek Him now had to leave their comfort zone and their grumbling behind if they were to find Him. God suggested to Moses that He would go with him, but Moses replied that if His presence didn't go with them, the journey was not one he wished to make.

And he said, My presence shall go with thee, and I will give thee rest. And he said unto him, If thy presence go not with me, carry us not up hence (Exodus 33:14–15).

Some are content living without His presence. They may be happy to sing about Him, but I want to sing to Him. I am not happy to just be where there is an anointing or gift in operation; I want to be where the glory of God is manifest. Moses had experienced supernatural interaction with God and was not ready to be absent from His glory. Moses then cried, "Show me Your glory."

And Moses said, I beseech thee, shew me Thy glory. And God said, I will make all my goodness pass before thee, and I will proclaim the name of the LORD before thee; and will be gracious to whom I will be gracious, and will shew mercy on whom I will shew mercy. And he said, Thou canst not see my face: for there shall no man see me, and live. And the

LORD said, Behold, there is a place by me, and thou shalt stand upon a rock: And it shall come to pass, while my glory passeth by, that I will put thee in a clift of the rock, and will cover thee with my hand while I pass by: And I will take away mine hand, and thou shalt see my back parts: but my face shall not be seen. (Exodus 33:19–23).

Sometimes you have to leave the company of others to move into the presence of God. Certainly this is a road less traveled. Often you have to shut the door behind you to those who are chasing a man or a ministry in order to find Him. This can be a lonely journey, but the reward is well worth it.

In thy presence is fulness of joy; at thy right hand there are pleasures for evermore (Psalm 16:11).

As I travel and minister, I often conduct what I call an "Abiding Presence" service. This is a time when I encourage congregations to join with me as we intentionally go past the anointing and seek the glorious presence of God. The rules are that no one receives prayer, no hands are laid on anyone, we do not ask God for anything, and we make no petitions or requests of Him. We must move beyond the anointing to walk into His glory. Under the anointing, a man will operate in his gift, give a word or share prophetic insight, which is usually as far as a service goes. Move past the anointing, and you will walk right into His presence.

I once conducted revival services in Ville Platte, Louisiana, where the pastor encouraged everyone to invite family members and friends as he anticipated seeing many people be healed. However, there was a slight problem. On my way to Louisiana, the Holy Spirit gave me specific instructions for the first service—I was not to lay hands on or pray for anyone. This was to be a time of only seeking God. It was extremely difficult to follow these directions because the anointing was so strong and the pastor had made promises to the people.

The best way I can describe this feeling of sitting on the anointing is like having a chocolate covered peanut in your mouth. Try holding the chocolate in your mouth until it dissolves without first crunching into the peanut. It is your natural tendency to want to crunch it. The same can be said when the anointing comes; those flowing in it feel like it is time to minister. But when God gives specific instructions, can you let the good pass you by, in order to receive the best?

In this service, I wanted to flow, to speak, to minister, but the command was clearly to "seek His face." I felt the pastor was extremely disappointed. I could see the letdown on people's faces, especially those who had driven great distances to be there, and then to have me say, "I won't be praying for anyone tonight." If I had been that pastor, I would have questioned my actions. I wondered whether anyone would return to the revival the second night. I could have proceeded to minister to folks to appease them and make the pastor happy, but I would have been disobedient to the Holy Spirit. I trusted I had made the right decision, but only time would tell.

The next night, I preached a message on miracles, and I opened the door for the supernatural presence of God to come in. The most amazing thing happened. The first night, we had passionately pursued Him. The second night, He aggressively pursued us! I saw some of the greatest miracles I have ever seen in my ministry, and it all happened so easily because we had tapped into the glory of God.

Imagine what would happen before a church service if intercessors were in one accord and prayed for His glory to come, rather than bringing Him our wish list. We need to start asking ourselves, *What does He want out of this time we spend together?* We must make the transition from just having our needs met and going home, to being a glorious Church. How can we be that glorious church if His glory is not present? More than another good service, we need His presence. You can live in His promise, protection, and provision without His presence, but why would you?

Chapter Nine

How To Carry Hot Coffee

It is written, Be ye holy; for I am holy (1 Peter 1:16).

Grass doesn't always have to be greener on the other side of the fence. Your grass could be just as green as theirs if you put forth the effort they have.

I am passionate about gardening. The small plot of ground behind my house produces more than enough fresh vegetables for my wife and me to comfortably live on during the entire year. Quite often, we even have last year's vegetables leftover in the freezer as fresh ones are harvested the following spring.

People often tell me, "Your ground is so blessed," and "Your soil is like the land flowing with milk and honey!" I simply laugh and tell them that my garden is no different from anyone else's soil. If other people would do what I do, they could grow what my garden produces, but only if they put forth the effort. I spend many hours working my ground to make my garden what it is. Blisters—something that many people don't like to get—are a necessary ingredient to a successful garden. The Lord will gladly do for you what He does for another, but only if you are willing to pay the price.

In the spiritual realm, God is ready to do good things in your life, but He doesn't just distribute spiritual blessings to those who are not in pursuit of Him. Salvation is a free gift, and it is available to all, but enjoying the depths of the blessings of God in your life is not determined by what God does but by what you do.

When something has cost you nothing, it is easy to place little value on it. If you come into a ministry or position that didn't cost you anything, you may get careless, and you could actually lose it, because you do not value it. In 2 Kings 6:5, the sons of the prophets were enlarging the house they were lodging in because it was too small. While one of the men was cutting down a tree, the axe head flew off the handle and landed in the water. It was important to get the axe head back because it was borrowed and he was responsible for it. When we have had to work for something, we tend to place a little more value on it than on something that belongs to someone else. Elisha took a stick and threw it in the water, and the ax head rose to the surface and the careless worker retrieved it.

Iron in the story of the axe head could refer to the presence of God in a man's life. In scripture, iron often refers to the glory of God. How does one carry the presence of God in his life and not lose it? The answer is, "very carefully," just like hot coffee. Because it did not come easy, it must be valued.

I took my daughters to a high school football game, and at half time we were in the middle of the usual crowd at the concessions stand. Everyone was pushing and shoving in line, trying to get their snacks before the second half began. My young daughter and I had stood in line for what seemed like an eternity. When we got near the front of the line, a very large man reached through the crowd and over our heads. He handed his friend in front of us money and asked him to pass him a cup of coffee. The man obliged, and I watched in horror as the cup filled with hot coffee passed above my daughter's face as she looked up. The force of the crowd caused his arm to begin to shake. I thought to myself, *If he spills that steaming cup on my daughter's face, I have no idea how I am going to react.* Fortunately, it never spilled on her, but it caused me to think about how a man carries his hot coffee.

A man carries a hot cup of coffee much differently than he carries a glass of ice-cold lemonade. A banker handles money from the vault much differently than when he plays Monopoly. A surgeon uses a little more caution during a surgery than he does when performing a procedure in the game of Operation. May I remind you, the church house is not a playhouse and the battleground is not a playground. How should we handle the things of God? The answer is, "very carefully."

When we serve God, we are required to walk in holiness if we desire to walk in a greater dimension. We must make sure we do things right. While in the wilderness, Moses and Aaron built the tabernacle and offered their first sacrifice upon the altar. Fire came from heaven and consumed the sacrifice. When the people saw it, they shouted and fell on their faces before God.

The next day, Aaron's two sons, who had been trained to do the work of the ministry, didn't do things according to the book, or the way they had seen it done previously. Men cannot cut a corner with God. What may not seem like much to us is viewed differently with God because He expects things done right. They offered what is referred to as "strange fire" to the Lord. God was not impressed, and fire went out from the sacrifice and burned them to ashes. There was nothing Aaron could say or do because God is a holy God, and His instructions were not followed.

And Nadab and Abihu, the sons of Aaron, took either of them his censer, and put fire therein, and put incense thereon, and offered strange fire before the Lord, which he commanded them not. And there went out fire from the Lord, and devoured them, and they died (Leviticus 10:1–2).

God is ready to release a revival, greater than anything we have ever seen at anyplace, anytime, or anywhere. To be a part of this revival, we must prepare much like Joshua had to prepare the children of Israel before they entered the Promised Land. All of Israel had to be on the same page, exactly as the Church must be of the same mind if we want to enjoy the blessing of the Lord.

God brought Israel into the Promised Land after forty years of wandering in the desert. The inhabitants of Canaan were afraid of Israel, but before God would use them in the conquest, He gave Joshua instructions to circumcise the males who had not yet been circumcised. Circumcision was a custom that began with Abraham 500 years before and was a sign upon the males that they were God's chosen people.

Joshua, along with many of the other men, had already been circumcised, but they were now commanded to circumcise all the males who had been born in the wilderness to prepare them for God's new purpose. For what they were being called to do, they could not take a chance on someone not being holy before the Lord.

In Joshua 3, God promised Israel He would do wonders among them "tomorrow." If you want to enjoy the fulfillment of the Lord's promise tomorrow, you must obey Him today. God had to have a fresh commitment from His people to walk in holiness before He would allow them to possess the land. The young men born in the wilderness, whom God was going to use to possess the land, had to be on the same page as the generation before them that God had brought out of Egypt, and that involved being circumcised.

> *The Lord said unto Joshua, Make thee sharp knives, and circumcise again the children of Israel the second time. And Joshua made him sharp knives, and circumcised the children of Israel at the hill of the foreskins. And this is the cause why Joshua did circumcise: All the people that came out of Egypt, that were males, even all the men of war, died in the wilderness by the way, after they came out of Egypt. Now all the people that came out were circumcised: but all the people that were born in the wilderness by the way as they came forth out of Egypt, them they had not circumcised* (Joshua 5:2–5).

People can get a little too comfortable in and around the atmosphere where the miraculous takes place. When you lose your awe, along with your determination to obey at any cost, you begin to make mistakes. God set the men down while their wounds healed to let them think about God's purpose for what He was about to allow them to do. You cannot rush off into battle and do great things for God without remembering that He is holy.

When the ark had been taken by the Philistines after Eli's death, the Philistines soon discovered that you do not treat the ark of the Lord as you would a common, ordinary trophy of war. It didn't take them long to send back the ark to Israel, returning it on a new cart pulled by oxen loaded with treasure.

After King Saul's death, David's first act as the newly crowned king was to bring the ark from Abinidab's house, where it had been stored, back to Jerusalem. While it was being transported, tragedy struck and a man died.

And they set the ark of God upon a new cart, and brought it out of the house of Abinadab that was in Gibeah: and Uzzah and Ahio, the sons of Abinadab, drave the new cart. And they brought it out of the house of Abinadab which was at Gibeah, accompanying the ark of God: and Ahio went before the ark. And David and all the house of Israel played before the Lord on all manner of instruments made of fir wood, even on harps, and on psalteries, and on timbrels, and on cornets, and on cymbals. And when they came to Nachon's threshingfloor, Uzzah put forth his hand to the ark of God, and took hold of it; for the oxen shook it. And the anger of the Lord was kindled against Uzzah; and God smote him there for his error; and there he died by the ark of God (2 Samuel 6:3–7).

Abinadab had two sons who had grown up around the "presence." The old box had been stored in the barn for safekeeping, and the two boys most likely had spent many afternoons playing around it the way that young boys would. Now, some years later, King David had come to retrieve it and had sent a new cart on which to transport it back to Jerusalem. The boys offered to go along for the journey and help since their dad was driving the cart. While making the journey, one of the oxen shook, the ark shifted, and appeared it would fall off the cart. Uzzah reached forth his hand to steady it and was instantly killed.

It had been a common, ordinary thing for the two boys to touch the box when they had played around it, but now it was different. When God is on the move, you handle things differently than when nothing is happening.

The Philistines handled the ark inappropriately by sending it back to Israel on a cart pulled by oxen. This made it appear to David that transporting it would be as easy as loading it up and hauling it away. As believers, we have been given instructions for handling what is holy. What works for unbelievers will never work for believers. This was not the way the Lord desired to be handled.

For because ye did it not at the first, the Lord our God made a breach upon us, for that we sought him not after the due order (1 Chronicles 15:13).

After the death of Uzzah, David went back and read the manual and realized the presence of God was to only be transported on the shoulders of godly men. What had worked for the unbeliever (the Philistines) would not work for them. Once the proper procedure was defined, transporting the ark was not a problem. Never let what God has established as holy, become common. What works for others will never work for us.

Miriam and Aaron, the older brother and sister of Moses, were about to find out that you don't treat baby brother like he is "baby brother." Moses had had an encounter with God in the wilderness and had been given a divine plan to deliver Israel from the oppression of Egypt. Pharaoh himself respected Moses as the messenger of God, but Moses' very own siblings could not see him in this new light.

And Miriam and Aaron spake against Moses because of the Ethiopian woman whom he had married: for he had married an Ethiopian woman. And they said, Hath the Lord indeed spoken only by Moses? hath he not spoken also by us? And the Lord heard it (Numbers 12:1–2).

Miriam and Aaron were probably not as upset about the Ethiopian wife Moses had married, as they were put out that "little brother" always seemed to be hearing from God and doing great things for Him. After all, they were older, and Miriam herself was the one who had helped Moses back into his mother's arms to be nursed after Pharaoh's daughter found him floating in the river. Miriam commented that the Lord had at times spoken through her and Aaron, as well.

Miriam's real issue was jealousy. She felt she needed a little attention too and tried to get people to side with her. Big Sister thought she should be equal to, or maybe even over, little brother, and she murmured that God could also speak through her and Aaron and not just Moses.

There was one small problem: Miriam had not been where "little brother" had been, nor had she paid the price he had paid. The bottom line was that God didn't trust her like He trusted Moses. She didn't see Moses as a man of God but only as her younger sibling. Miriam was smitten with leprosy and was put outside the camp for seven days. Being the older sister, she was most likely the instigator, and God dealt more harshly with her than with Aaron, who had a reputation for being a follower.

Problems arise in churches when people lose respect for God's man. The pastor may have even been raised around them from childhood, and he may have come from among them into his God-called position of leadership. Other issues arise when those called to serve faithfully under a pastor in a supportive role feel like they should have the same authority as the pastor with the same respect from the people.

Oftentimes strife will develop between a worship leader and a pastor over control and who gets credit. Lucifer himself, the original worship leader in heaven, attempted to overthrow God and to sit upon the throne that belonged only to Him, desiring the attention God received.

May I remind you, other than Lucifer, Miriam was the first worship leader mentioned in the Bible. Not only was she a musician and dancer, but she also was identified as being a prophetess, one who could see in advance the wonderful works of God that the Israelites were being led into. Often those with an anointing or talent feel that they do not receive the proper recognition due them. Rather than appreciate where God has placed them and support God's leader over them, they are tempted by the deceiver to promote themselves. They can also feel that no one has properly recognized their gifting or given them the respect they feel they deserve. May I remind you, Numbers 12:3 states that "Moses himself was very meek, above all the men which were upon the face of the earth."

When men rise up out of disrespect for God's man, it shows what kind of people they are, and it indicates why God, up to that point in their lives, has not chosen them for the position of influence they pursue. When a man like Moses, rather than retaliate, will trust God and love people, it demonstrates exactly why God chose him and why they are in the position they now occupy.

You would think everyone would learn by Miriam's experience, but people seldom do. It didn't matter that Moses withstood Pharoah with his rod, brought the plagues against Egypt, parted the Red Sea, or caused water to flow from the rock, he was again about to be challenged.

Not long after Miriam and Aaron challenged Moses' authority, he was challenged again. His first challenge came from his own house, but the second challenge came from one of the princes, a bright and rising star from among Israel. His name was Korah, and he led a rebellion that was aimed at both Moses and Aaron.

> *Now Korah…and Dathan and Abiram…took men…. And they rose up before Moses, with certain of the children of Israel, two hundred and fifty princes of the assembly, famous in the congregation, men of renown: And they gathered themselves together against Moses and against Aaron, and said unto them, Ye take too much upon you, seeing all the congregation are holy, every one of them, and the Lord is among them: wherefore then lift ye up yourselves above the congregation of the Lord? And when Moses heard it, he fell upon his face* (Numbers 16:1–4).

Korah judged himself to be holy, and he accused Moses and Aaron of promoting themselves before the people. He suggested that he and others were able to lead as effectively as the two of them. Korah gathered all the children of Israel at the door of the tabernacle in a rebellion, and God simply told Moses and Aaron to stand back.

> *And Korah gathered all the congregation against them unto the door of the tabernacle of the congregation: and the glory of the Lord appeared unto all the congregation. And the Lord spake unto Moses and unto Aaron, saying, Separate yourselves from among this congregation, that I may consume them in a moment. And they fell upon their faces, and said, O God, the God of the spirits of all flesh, shall one man sin, and wilt thou be wroth with all the congregation?* (verses 19–22)

> *And Moses said, Hereby ye shall know that the Lord hath sent me to do all these works; for I have not done them of mine own mind. If these men die the common death of all men, or if they be visited after the visitation of all men; then the Lord hath not sent me. But if the Lord make*

a new thing, and the earth open her mouth, and swallow them up, with all that appertain unto them, and they go down quick into the pit; then ye shall understand that these men have provoked the Lord. And it came to pass, as he had made an end of speaking all these words, that the ground clave asunder that was under them: And the earth opened her mouth, and swallowed them up, and their houses, and all the men that appertained unto Korah, and all their goods. They, and all that appertained to them, went down alive into the pit, and the earth closed upon them: and they perished from among the congregation. And all Israel that were round about them fled at the cry of them: for they said, Lest the earth swallow us up also (verses 28–34).

God took Korah, and all those who stood with him, completely out of the picture. God warned the people to separate themselves from him, and those who did not would perish with the same fate. The ground opened up and swallowed Korah and all he possessed. God took him out in an instant, and it was as if he had never existed. God's chosen man will always outlast those who stand against him. The Lord told Moses in Exodus 14:14, "The Lord shall fight for you, and ye shall hold your peace."

Rebellions today, as well as then, all begin at the door of the House of God. People who are often themselves princes among the people, the very ones who are rising stars, have the greatest tendency to forget that this is the Lord's Church. People forget who they are and the position they are to fill. It is easy, especially when people get tired, discouraged, or disgruntled, or if they feel like they have not been recognized, to forget they must remain holy and do things right. God will promote them if and when He decides they are ready.

God's presence will only increase in our lives and ministry when the proper respect and awe are given to Him and to others appointed by Him. When we lose our sense of awe and think it is for us, by us, or about us, He either removes Himself or He removes us. The children of Israel, though they got discouraged and complained at times, never again entertained another rebellion after God dealt decisively with Korah.

You can enjoy this wonderful Christian life that so many others are experiencing but only when you do it right and keep things holy. You can be as blessed as anyone else. You do not have to stand back in envy and boast you could do something great for God if you had it as easy as someone else has had it. If you are preparing to run with your second wind, there are no shortcuts, no easy paths. You may never know what others have had to do to get to where they are. When God pours out His Spirit in a global fashion, you can be a part of it, but only if you are holy. How are you going to carry your hot coffee?

Chapter Ten

When the Milk Cows Come Home

Lo, we have left all, and followed thee (Luke 18:28).

During a trip to conduct revival services in Andrews, Texas, I received an invitation to hold an impartation/healing service on a Sunday afternoon in Monahans. I shared with the pastor who had invited me that my first obligation was to the pastor in Andrews, but if he were willing to release us for the afternoon, I would be more than glad to minister. We were released to go, and the hunger-filled church was packed with people. Following the preaching of the Word, Johnny Knight, who was with me on this trip providing music, joined me in the altar area and we ministered to the crowd. The altar service became lengthy as people sought the Lord. In order to be able to leave so we could make it back on time to Andrews for the evening service, we lined the people up and prayed our way out the front door.

Earlier while I was preaching, I had noticed a young man come in and sit on the front row. I later learned the he was the pastor of a local Spirit-filled church. Since Johnny and I needed to leave, I felt the Lord say, "Put this young man and his wife in charge." This was such a strange request because this was not even his church where we were ministering, and the actual pastor was standing close by. Something about this young couple had captured my attention, even though I knew nothing about them other than that they appeared to be hungry for more of the Lord.

I heard reports after the service that this pastor and wife had received an anointing that day under which they had never operated before, and the service continued on even though I was not there. God's touch on their lives has now grown to such a magnitude that they have been interviewed on television and have even published a book. They are regularly asked to speak at conferences and to conduct revivals, and you will often see unique miracles in their services. I continue to be inspired by this pastor who travels with me on occasion and has ministered in my church when he is available. When God's presence touches lives, amazing and unusual things begin to happen. The question becomes, "Is it God or is it just coincidence?"

There are few things I love more than a Spirit-filled altar service. I love to be around people who are oblivious to time, seeking God, and rejoicing when His presence comes. This is the atmosphere in which supernatural things happen—the kind of things no one will talk about but just ponder in their hearts. Things that, if told to the wrong people, will cause you to be labeled "crazy."

When His presence comes, it touches people and it often manifests in amazing ways. You may see people shouting, running, dancing, and shaking. Other people may experience extreme heat or a cool wind or smell a heavenly fragrance. Still others feel the current of an invisible river swirling around their legs, or their body may freeze into a position, making them unable to move while God works inside them. You may see people lying still on the floor, and then others may manifest nothing at all. There could be people laughing, rejoicing, or just sitting silent while someone next to them sobs uncontrollably.

When I conduct an altar service in which I detect the supernatural presence of God, I never like to see the flesh manifest itself. The flesh is not always acting in a manner that would bring attention to oneself. When that kind of flesh is seen, it is easy to deal with. The flesh that I most often see is when people genuinely and truly feel the stirring of the Spirit, but they resist it for fear of losing control or appearing undignified before other people. It is common to sense someone resisting when the Spirit begins a work in them. When I become aware of it, I reassure people, just relax, let go, and trust the Spirit to work inside of them.

As a pastor, I always watch to see how people are moved by the

Spirit and what their reactions are. When the Spirit moves and people react to it, the question many people have is, "Is it the flesh, or is it really God?" It has been my question as well.

We can look into the book of Samuel for an answer to this question. The Philistines had come to Ebenezer and taken the ark of the Lord from the tabernacle to the Philistine city of Ashdod. In this story, Eli, the high priest, fell over backward, his neck was broken, and he died; his two sons were killed; his pregnant daughter-in-law died in childbirth; and the boy, Ichabod, was born. Ichabod means, "The glory is departed."

The moment the Philistines took the ark of the Lord, strange and abnormal events occurred wherever it was taken. When the ark was placed next to Dagon in his temple, in the morning their priests would find Dagon toppled facedown on the floor. Dagon would be placed back in its upright position again, but the next morning they would find it facedown once more. Eventually, the head and palms of the hands were broken off. The priests of Dagon became terrified and refused to go back into their temple. The ark was then transported to city after city, and everywhere it was taken, the same strange phenomena happened.

And the Philistines took the ark of God, and brought it from Ebenezer unto Ashdod. When the Philistines took the ark of God, they brought it into the house of Dagon, and set it by Dagon. And when they of Ashdod arose early on the morrow, behold, Dagon was fallen upon his face to the earth before the ark of the Lord. And they took Dagon, and set him in his place again. And when they arose early on the morrow morning, behold, Dagon was fallen upon his face to the ground before the ark of the Lord; and the head of Dagon and both the palms of his hands were cut off upon the threshold; only the stump of Dagon was left to him. Therefore neither the priests of Dagon, nor any that come into Dagon's house, tread on the threshold of Dagon in Ashdod unto this day (1 Samuel 5:1–5).

But the hand of the Lord was heavy upon them of Ashdod, and he destroyed them, and smote them with emerods, even Ashdod and the coasts thereof. And when the men of Ashdod saw that it was so, they said, The ark of the God of Israel shall not abide with us: for his hand is sore upon us, and upon Dagon our god. They sent therefore and gathered all the lords of the Philistines unto them, and said, What shall we do with the ark of the God of Israel? And they answered, Let the ark of the God of Israel be carried about unto Gath. And they carried the ark of the God of Israel about thither. And it was so, that, after they had carried it about, the hand of the Lord was against the city with a very great destruction: and he smote the men of the city, both small and great, and they had emerods in their secret parts. Therefore they sent the ark of God to Ekron. And it came to pass, as the ark of God came to Ekron, that the Ekronites cried out, saying, They have brought about the ark of the God of Israel to us, to slay us and our people. So they sent and gathered to-gether all the lords of the Philistines, and said, Send away the ark of the God of Israel, and let it go again to his own place, that it slay us not, and our people: for there was a deadly destruction throughout all the city; the hand of God was very heavy there. And the men that died not were smitten with the emerods: and the cry of the city went up to heaven (1 Samuel 5:6–12).

The Philistines' lords were brought together and asked a very important question by the rulers of the villages: "Is it really the God of Israel and His hand against us, or were the unusual events simply a co-incidence?"

The lords of the Philistines devised a plan and suggested they should take two milk cows that had never been fit with a harness, hook them up to a cart that they had never seen, pull it down a road they had never traveled, to a place they had never been. If the two milk cows walked directly to Bethshemesh, a location just inside Israel's border, and did not turn to the right or to the left, it could be said that Israel's God was at work against them. The plan was put into action and the results were amazing.

Now therefore make a new cart, and take two [milk cows], on which there hath come no yoke, and tie the [cows] to the cart, and bring their calves home from them: And take the ark of the Lord, and lay it upon the cart; and put the jewels of gold, which ye return him for a trespass of-

fering, in a coffer by the side thereof; and send it away, that it may go. And see, if it goeth up by the way of his own coast to Bethshemesh, then he hath done us this great evil: but if not, then we shall know that it is not his hand that smote us: it was a chance that happened to us. The men did so; and took two [milk cows], and tied them to the cart, and shut up their calves at home: And they laid the ark of the Lord upon the cart.... And the [cows] took the straight way to the way of Beth-shemesh, and went along the highway, lowing as they went, and turned not aside to the right hand or to the left (1 Samuel 6:7–12).

The two milk cows took their journey despite the fact that their calves, which they had been nursing, were bellowing. In spite of the cries from the calves, the cows never looked back or waivered in their journey and went straight ahead to Bethshemesh. The cows went down the middle of the highway, lowing as they went. (Lowing is the sound a cow makes when it is content.)

This method the Philistines used is interesting and the same test can be applied when determining if a persons' different behavior is genuine or just a coincidence. If God is really at work in a person's life, they can be yoked together with God and carry a cross. They can walk with God, alongside others, down a path which they have never before travelled and not look to the right or left, to a predetermined destination they have never been to. They will be content even though their friends and affections they have walked away from keep trying to beckon them back.

When a person finds the one thing they have been looking for, the thing that satisfies them, they will turn their back on everything they have ever known to walk in their new life. When God begins to do amazing things in someone's life, sometimes family members and friends may begin to say they liked him better the old way. I have found that what God does in a person's life often makes them more enemies than friends.

And they of Bethshemesh were reaping their wheat harvest in the valley: and they lifted up their eyes, and saw the ark, and rejoiced to see it. And the cart came into the field of Joshua, a Beth-shemite, and stood there, where there was a great stone: and they clave the wood of the cart, and offered the [cows] a burnt offering unto the Lord. And the Levites took down the ark of the Lord, and the coffer that was with it, wherein the jewels of gold were, and put them on the great stone: and the men of Bethshemesh offered burnt offerings and sacrificed sacrifices (1 Samuel 6: 13–15).

Don't think for a moment that everyone is going to celebrate with you. Friends and family might even "crucify you." When the two milk cows brought back the ark of the Presence and stopped in the field of Joshua, the men working in the fields saw what happened and appeared to be happy. The cows were then brought to a place in the field where there was a great stone, the cart was broken into pieces and set on fire, and the cows were offered for a sacrifice.

Turning from a life of sin to live a life pleasing to God is the most fulfilling event that can take place in a person's life. The old nature and mindset has to change, or you will quickly be drawn back into the very thing that Christ brought you out of. Old friends will try to figure you out and will often say, "Just give them a little time, and it will run its course." Even mature believers in the Church who should be encouraging others will often say, "They probably won't make it."

Peter said, Lo, we have left all, and followed thee. And he said unto them, Verily I say unto you, There is no man that hath left house, or parents, or brethren, or wife, or children, for the kingdom of God's sake, Who shall not receive manifold more in this present time, and in the world to come life everlasting (Luke 18:28–30).

Saul, the Christian-hater, who later became a great apostle, had the same problem. He had a reputation for killing Christians and was on his way from Jerusalem to Damascus to arrest any who professed Christ. As he traveled on the road to Damascus, the Lord met him and transformed his life. Although Saul knew he was a different man, it took time for other believers to trust him. It was only after the Lord told Ananias to lay hands on Saul and pray for his blindness that he himself trusted Saul's conversion.

Then Ananias answered, Lord, I have heard by many of this man, how much evil he hath done to thy saints at Jerusalem: And here he hath authority from the chief priests to bind all that call on thy name (Acts 9:13–14).

Saul, whose name was changed to Paul, became one of the greatest apostles in the early church. Although Paul was often beaten, stoned, and falsely accused, his faith in God never faltered. It was while he was in prison for preaching the Gospel that he wrote most of his New Testament epistles. The Bible does not tell us of the death of Paul; the last we read of him is in a prison cell in Rome. Tradition tells us that Paul was beheaded for his faith in Christ and for preaching the Gospel he believed.

For I am not ashamed of the gospel of Christ: for it is the power of God unto salvation to every one that believeth; to the Jew first, and also to the Greek (Romans 1:16).

The next time someone comes to you and questions, "Is this really God, or is it just you?" do not argue with them; let your integrity and your fruit speak for you. If you are preparing to run with your second wind, you must be prepared to make whatever change is needed in your life and never look back. If it is really God inside of you, you will gladly do it.

Chapter Eleven

Keep Watering the Camels

I will draw water for thy camels also, until they have done drinking (Genesis 24:19).

God wants His children to prosper. Prosperity can be defined as good things that happen in our lives: a promotion on the job, an inheritance, good health, or an increase in finances. It may also come in the form of the car that never has trouble, appliances that never need repair, bargains at the department store, or children who never need to see the doctor.

Let the Lord be magnified, which hath pleasure in the prosperity of his servant (Psalm 35:27).

Even in the face of opposition, God will show His favor by turning what was meant to be a curse into a blessing. I often tell those who need a breakthrough, "If it were easy, everybody would be doing it." Those who quit because of the trial involved will never see the fullness of the blessing of the Lord.

The Lord thy God turned the curse into a blessing unto thee (Deuteronomy 23:5).

The Word of God is filled with examples of people who endured a trial to obtain the promise. Joseph spent years in an Egyptian prison before his promotion. Moses endured forty years on the back side of the

Arabian desert before getting his instructions. Daniel prayed in spite of those who opposed him and was promoted to prominence in the court of the Babylonians.

The most noted character in the Bible is, of course, Jesus. God did not choose to send Him to earth to live in a plush palace, born to a royal family. Jesus was sent to the arms of a mother who had lost her reputation because of the rumors surrounding her pregnancy.

Jesus' life was one of sorrow. There was no other way He would be able to fulfill the Father's purpose for His life. He had to experience rejection, suffering, and pain, yet He was faithful unto death. Because of Jesus' faithfulness, He gives hope to all who put their trust in Him.

> *He hath no form nor comeliness; and when we shall see him, there is no beauty that we should desire him. He is despised and rejected of men; a man of sorrows, and acquainted with grief: and we hid as it were our faces from him; he was despised, and we esteemed him not* (Isaiah 53:2–3).

> *Looking unto Jesus the author and finisher of our faith; who for the joy that was set before him endured the cross, despising the shame, and is set down at the right hand of the throne of God* (Hebrews 12:2).

It is not possible for a man to obtain his crown except he bear his cross. If God did not spare His own Son, we can rest assured, there will also be a price that we must pay. The manner in which one stands the test will determine the magnitude of his blessing.

> *He that spared not his own Son, but delivered him up for us all...*(Romans 8:32).

Enduring hardship may be part of the process in receiving a blessing. It doesn't bother God to ask someone to do something outside their comfort zone. Naaman came to Elisha after he heard the prophet was able to work miracles. He expected Elisha to simply wave his hand or make a great speech, and then he would be healed. On the contrary, Elisha only sent a message and told Naaman to go and dip seven times in the Jordan River. At first Naaman was quite offended, but he was eventually convinced by his servant that it was not too much to ask.

Even though it was a humbling experience because of his status as captain of the Syrian army, he obeyed the man of God and was completely healed.

God made a promise to Abraham: "Surely blessing I will bless thee, and multiplying I will multiply thee. And so, after he had patiently endured, he obtained the promise" (Hebrews 6:14–15). The promise was so big that it would take all of history for it to be fulfilled. As a matter of fact, all of recorded biblical history revolves around the story and this promise.

Now the Lord had said unto Abram, Get thee out of thy country, and from thy kindred, and from thy father's house, unto a land that I will shew thee: And I will make of thee a great nation, and I will bless thee, and make thy name great; and thou shalt be a blessing: And I will bless them that bless thee, and curse him that curseth thee: and in thee shall all families of the earth be blessed (Genesis 12:1–3).

Abraham's wife, Sarah, had died, and he knew he would soon follow as he was very old. To be sure that Isaac did not marry a Canaanite woman, Abraham sent his most trusted servant to Haran in search of a wife for his son. This was the same place where Abraham had found his own wife many years before. Abraham entrusted all of his wealth into his servant's custody and instructed him to use these resources in whatever way necessary to convince a special young lady to leave her family and marry a man she had never met.

And Abraham was old, and well stricken in age: and the Lord had blessed Abraham in all things. And Abraham said unto his eldest servant of his house, that ruled over all that he had, Put, I pray thee, thy hand under my thigh: And I will make thee swear by the Lord, the God of heaven, and the God of the earth, that thou shalt not take a wife unto my son of the daughters of the Canaanites, among whom I dwell: But thou shalt go unto my country, and to my kindred, and take a wife unto my son Isaac. And the servant said unto him, Peradventure the woman will not be willing to follow me unto this land: must I needs bring thy son again unto the land from whence thou camest? And Abraham said unto him, Beware thou that thou bring not my son thither again. The

Lord God of heaven, which took me from my father's house, and from the land of my kindred, and which spake unto me, and that sware unto me, saying, Unto thy seed will I give this land; he shall send his angel before thee, and thou shalt take a wife unto my son from thence. And if the woman will not be willing to follow thee, then thou shalt be clear from this my oath: only bring not my son thither again. And the servant put his hand under the thigh of Abraham his master, and sware to him concerning that matter (Genesis 24:1–9).

The servant journeyed to Nahor, a city in Mesopotamia, and stopped at the village well. He arrived about the time the maidens gathered in the evening to draw water. After giving orders for the camels to kneel, he began to pray. Not wishing to waste time, he asked God to have the damsel, who was to marry Isaac, offer to draw water for his camels.

The servant had not yet finished praying when a young lady with a pitcher on her shoulder gave him water to drink and offered to water the camels. She carried the water she had drawn to the trough and gave them as much as they were able to drink.

And the servant took ten camels of the camels of his master, and departed; for all the goods of his master were in his hand: and he arose, and went to Mesopotamia, unto the city of Nahor. And he made his camels to kneel down without the city by a well of water at the time of the evening, even the time that women go out to draw water. And he said, O Lord God of my master Abraham, I pray thee, send me good speed this day, and shew kindness unto my master Abraham.

Behold, I stand here by the well of water; and the daughters of the men of the city come out to draw water: And let it come to pass, that the damsel to whom I shall say, Let down thy pitcher, I pray thee, that I may drink; and she shall say, Drink, and I will give thy camels drink also: let the same be she that thou hast appointed for thy servant Isaac; and thereby shall I know that thou hast shewed kindness unto my master.

And it came to pass, before he had done speaking, that, behold, Rebekah came out…with her pitcher upon her shoulder. And the damsel was very fair to look upon, a virgin, neither had any man known her: and she went down to the well, and filled her pitcher, and came up. And the servant ran to meet her, and said, Let me, I pray thee, drink a little water of thy pitcher. And she said, Drink, my lord: and she hasted, and let down her pitcher upon her hand, and gave him drink. And when she had done giving him drink, she said, I will draw water for thy camels also, until they have done drinking. And she hasted, and emptied her pitcher into the trough, and ran again unto the well to draw water, and drew for all his camels. And the man wondering at her held his peace, to wit whether the Lord had made his journey prosperous or not. And it came to pass, as the camels had done drinking, that the man took a golden earring of half a shekel weight, and two bracelets for her hands of ten shekels weight of gold (Genesis 24:10–22).

The servant was pleased because God had quickly made it known that he should make her the offer of marriage to Isaac. This young lady, named Rebekah, was a very beautiful girl. The Bible mentions that she was a virgin and no man had ever known her. This was an important quality because she was not one to appear overly friendly, especially to a strange man. Not only was she beautiful and well-mannered, but she was also a diligent worker. She did not rest until all the stranger's camels were watered.

The servant explained to Rebekah's father how Abraham had given him specific orders to find Isaac a wife, and how, after prayer, God had quickly showed him favor with her. He then opened the treasure that each camel carried and gave Rebekah silver, gold, and fine clothes. With these gifts came a promise that where she was going, she would be well provided for. He presented to her family many precious things as well.

And now if ye will deal kindly and truly with my master, tell me: and if not, tell me; that I may turn to the right hand, or to the left. Then Laban and Bethuel answered and said, the thing proceedeth from the Lord: we cannot speak unto thee bad or good. Behold, Rebekah is before thee, take her, and go, and let her be thy master's son's wife, as the Lord hath spoken. And it came to pass, that, when Abraham's servant heard their words, he worshipped the Lord, bowing himself to the earth. And

the servant brought forth jewels of silver, and jewels of gold, and rai-
ment, and gave them to Rebekah: he gave also to her brother and to her
mother precious things (Genesis 24:49–53).

After her family received the gifts, they called Rebekah and asked
her what she would like to do. Rebekah accepted the gracious proposal
for marriage to Isaac, and her family blessed her, saying, "May you be
the mother of thousands of millions."

And they called Rebekah, and said unto her, Wilt thou go with this
man? And she said, I will go. And they sent away Rebekah their sister,
and her nurse, and Abraham's servant, and his men. And they blessed
Rebekah, and said unto her, Thou art our sister, be thou the mother of
thousands of millions, and let thy seed possess the gate of those which hate
them (Genesis 24:58–60).

Rebekah and her maidens made the journey back to Canaan, and
the "vehicle of choice" that Abraham's servant provided for her was a
camel. Isaac took Rebekah to be his wife, and he loved her.

And Rebekah arose, and her damsels, and they rode upon the camels, and
followed the man: and the servant took Rebekah, and went his way....
And Isaac went out to meditate in the field at the eventide: and he lifted
up his eyes, and saw, and, behold, the camels were coming. And Rebekah
lifted up her eyes, and when she saw Isaac, she lighted off the camel
(Genesis 24:61–64).

And the servant told Isaac all things that he had done. And Isaac
brought her into his mother Sarah's tent, and took Rebekah, and she be-
came his wife; and he loved her: and Isaac was comforted after his
mother's death (Genesis 24:66–67).

How unfitting for Rebekah, who had such a promising future as the
wife of the child of promise, the promised mother of thousands of millions, to be carried to her destiny on a nasty camel.

Who would ever believe that a destiny could be changed simply by
offering water to camels that belonged to a total stranger? Drawing
water was no small task, as each camel had the ability to hold forty gal-

lons of water. There were ten camels, and the Scripture says they drank until they were filled. It is possible that Rebekah drew as much as 400 gallons of water.

Camels are among the most unpleasant animals to be around. Their odor is obnoxious; horses can't even stand to be near them. They are ugly, cantankerous creatures who offer a very uncomfortable ride. Having a mind of their own, they are known to be the most stubborn and dangerous of the so-called tame animals. Camels have three unpleasant habits that present a challenge to anyone wanting to ride one: they inflict a very painful bite, they spit, and they kick.

For royalty, or people with wealth, horses were the chosen vehicle of transportation. However, for someone taking a very long journey, camels were more durable and could travel when horses would soon grow fatigued. Camels eat anything readily available and thrive in arid conditions. They have been known to store enough water inside their hump to last an entire dry season.

Now, these are interesting facts, but you are not reading this chapter to learn about the characteristics of camels. However, there are types and pictures represented here that will help you as you pursue your own destiny.

Rebekah represents the ones who are willing to forsake all and follow Christ to become His Bride. This is a journey of faith because those who take it can be sure of nothing other than the promises the servant has made to them. Having been given an earnest when the journey began, these are promised great reward when they finally arrive at their destination.

Camels represent the vehicle God uses to bring you into renewal. The goal of the believer is not revival, another wave of the Spirit, or a spiritual gift. The Church, which involves the fivefold ministry, is God's vehicle that takes us into spiritual maturity.

Camels were chosen for the journey because they were durable and could outdistance any other vehicle of that day. Camels also do not have the ability to back up; they can only go forward. This was fitting because what God does in a person's life will always take them forward. Some people balk at advancing and often try to regress. Simply said, "You cannot live on yesterday's blessing."

The trusted servant represents the Holy Spirit, sent to find and prepare a Bride for Christ. Those who have chosen to follow Christ, in a sense, travel blind because they only know what the Spirit has revealed to them. Those who have taken the journey have been given a heavenly earnest, and a greater reward has been promised when they are later joined to "Isaac."

> *In whom ye also trusted, after that ye heard the word of truth, the gospel of your salvation: in whom also after that ye believed, ye were sealed with that holy Spirit of promise, Which is the earnest of our inheritance until the redemption of the purchased possession, unto the praise of his glory* (Ephesians 1:13–14).

Isaac represents the fullness of everything believed and hoped for in Christ. To be joined to Him and live forever in His presence is the goal of every believer when they begin their journey of faith. When the camel Rebekah was riding took her to where Isaac was, she instantly knew it was him, and she quickly dismounted. It was worth the long, grueling journey after just one glimpse of Isaac. A walk of faith is always taken on a road of uncertainty. Until the moment she saw Isaac, Rebekah could not be certain that everything told her was accurate.

> *And Rebekah lifted up her eyes, and when she saw Isaac, she lighted off the camel* (Genesis 24:64).

The Holy Spirit desires to give us all the gifts the Father has for us, but many times we get offended at the manner in which He brings us to them. As the Bride, if we are going to receive what has been promised to us, we cannot be offended at how God does it. Rebekah rode a camel to obtain her promise. As believers, we must carry our cross to receive a crown.

Following Christ certainly has its setbacks. The vehicle God has designed to take us from being a new believer to becoming mature Christian is the Church. The Church is obviously not a place that has been perfected; it's a work in progress. As long as you are around people, even God's people, there is the potential to be disappointed, disillusioned, let down, and misunderstood. Serving God would be easy for many if faithfulness, commitment, and giving were not expected.

Personal and corporate revival is a wonderful experience. Yet, as I stated in a previous chapter, when God moves in a person's life, he often gains more enemies than friends. People may label him "crazy." But with the increase of spiritual activity in his life, an incredible amount of joy comes that cannot be found elsewhere. Some will not understand his newfound happiness, and it may cause them to walk away.

Pastors say they want revival because it brings energy. When the Spirit comes, the Church is filled with life, which produces effective evangelism and draws visitors and larger crowds. Happy people are giving people. There will be a noticeable difference in the areas of stewardship, commitment, and Christian service.

Revival does bring a boost of life to a church but is not without its challenges. Revival creates as many problems as it solves. Anytime there is growth in a church, older members may feel they are losing their position or influence. Strangers are taking the seats of people who may have sat in that pew for years. Mature believers are expected to step up and take on new areas of service. The excitement might attract the "wrong" kind or another culture of people, making older members feel uneasy.

If a person wants to enter into the fullness of a promise, it involves stretching. One must turn loose of outdated methods and seek newer, more effective ones. In the terms of a wineskin, we must remain pliable or we will soon crack and lose the precious contents.

For Rebekah, the journey from Nahor to Canaan would not be an easy one. Her transition from being a young girl into a mother of promise certainly possessed the potential to make her want to quit. She was on a camel, and the camel was not taking her back to where she came from. We can be confident that, on her long journey, she must have had her share of bites, spits, and kicks. Still, there was no other way but to ride the camel.

Serving God may have brought you pain, ridicule, and disappointment. You may have wondered, *Doesn't He care? And, if He does care, why doesn't He help me?* Many have applauded the decision you made, but they have remained behind so that you have to make the journey alone. The road is a long, hard one and often you are tempted to go back. For the joy of the reward, you remain on the camel and endure the bites, spits, and kicks, along with the blisters. All this could have been avoided if you had never watered the camels.

I make regular trips to Ireland to bring words of encouragement to pastors and congregations. Before one of these trips, a pastor friend, Richard W. Cleghorn, called me and said, "I just feel I need to give you a word." He shared the story of Isaac, Rebekah, the camel, and the promise. As he spoke, the Holy Spirit said, "This is a word for a particular pastor in Ireland."

This was not a message I had ever preached, so I was unsure how effective it would be. After arriving in Ireland, I delivered the message to the church. As I shared the word, the pastor became engulfed by waves of the Spirit of God. I thought to myself, *Wow! That must have been some mighty fine preaching!*

After the service I discovered the truth of the matter. Several years before, the Lord had made this pastor a promise. As the church moved into a season of renewal, they began to be ridiculed by Christians who did not like or understand what they saw. All sense of dignity and respect was taken from them, leaving them severely hurt and very discouraged. The promise the Lord had given the pastor involved the "treasure" being delivered on a camel. My word for the pastor that night was, "If you don't want the treasure, quit watering the camels."

When the service was over, the pastor told me she had purchased a wooden camel, which stood about four feet tall. It had been placed on the platform to remind the congregation of a promise that God had made to them only a few years before. The promise, given to the pastor, involved a treasure coming, like it did to Rebekah, on a stinking camel.

A month before I brought this word to them, an intercessor visiting the church seemed to be bothered by what she saw. She embarrassed the pastor publicly by suggesting that the camel had been made into an idol, and that it should be removed from the church immediately. This pastor was very puzzled as to why God would make a promise, and then through an outsider, tell her something very different. The pastor never removed the camel from the church, but it was placed behind a curtain so no one would easily see it.

My word for the pastor after speaking of Isaac, Rebekah, and specifically the camel was, "If you don't want the treasure, quit watering the camels." Now, I understood. It was not my preaching that had moved the pastor, but it was a reminder from God that He will always keep a promise He makes.

There will be those who are well meaning, but they do not understand what God has told you. After I delivered this message, the pastor brought the camel out from the obscure place where it had been hidden and placed it again in full view. Seeing the camel is a continual reminder to them that the promises of God are true and will come to pass.

Don't give up your God-given dream. His promises to you will come to pass. One day the pain you endured by remaining faithful will bring you to your great reward. If you want your promise to come true…keep watering the camels.

Chapter Twelve

When You Don't Have a Leg to Stand On

[King] Asa…was diseased in his feet…yet in his disease he sought not to the Lord, but to the physicians (2 Chronicles 16:12).

It seems a vast majority of Christians have a hard time believing God can heal. Even though God's Word is clear on the subject, too many have been brought up in an environment where they have been taught that it only happened in early Church history, but it does not happen today.

Since the Garden of Eden, where the Fall of man initially took place, God has had a remedy for sin and every disease known to mankind.

…the Lamb slain from the foundation of the world (Revelation 13:8).

But he was wounded for our transgressions, he was bruised for our iniquities: the chastisement of our peace was upon him; and with his stripes we are healed (Isaiah 53:5).

How great are his signs! and how mighty are his wonders! his kingdom is an everlasting kingdom, and his dominion is from generation to generation (Daniel 4:3).

Jesus Christ the same yesterday, and to day, and for ever (Hebrews 13:8).

A lady I once offered to pray for responded to me by saying, "I am sorry, but I do not see the Bible the way you see it." I replied, "It is not how I see it, but I am simply believing what Jesus said." Jesus' words should not be open for debate. Personally, I have seen too many miracles to make me quit believing that healing is for today. Remember, a man with a testimony is never at the mercy of a man with just an opinion.

Why are so many filled with unbelief? Why is it hard for them to believe? Jesus Himself encountered a city where nothing would happen: In Nazareth, "...he did not many mighty works there because of their unbelief" (Matthew 13:58). I have heard people say, "When I see it, I will believe it." My attitude is, "If I believe it, I will see it."

The demonstration of the power of God is available today as it was for the prophets of old. I would rather believe God and have nothing happen than not give Him a chance to move on my behalf. You never know what will happen when you turn your faith into action. In chapter five, I referred to the blind man in Jericho. Bartimaeus decided he had nothing to lose. People may ask you when you tell them that you are believing God for a miracle, "What if nothing happens?" I suggest you reply to them, "What if it does?" There is nothing too hard for God.

Ah Lord God! behold, thou hast made the heaven and the earth by thy great power and stretched out arm, and there is nothing too hard for thee (Jeremiah 32:17).

People often live far below the level of blessing that has already been provided for in Christ. One does not have to believe in divine healing to go to heaven, but wouldn't it be disheartening to eventually arrive and find out you had access to so much more?

The story is told of an eighty-five-year-old couple who, having been married almost sixty years, died in a car crash. They had been in good health the last ten years mainly due to the wife's interest in health food and exercise.

When they reached the Pearly Gates, Saint Peter took them to their mansion, which was decked out with a beautiful kitchen and master bath suite complete with Jacuzzi. As they oohed and aahed, the old man asked Peter how much all this was going to cost. "It's free," Peter replied. "This is heaven."

Next they went out back to survey the championship golf course that backed up to the home. They would have golfing privileges every day, and each week the course changed to a new one representing the great golf courses on earth. The old man asked, "What are the green fees?" Peter's reply, "This is heaven; you play for free."

Next they went to the clubhouse and saw the lavish buffet lunch with the cuisines of the world laid out. "How much to eat?" asked the old man. "Don't you understand yet? This is heaven—it is free!" Peter replied with some exasperation.

"Well, where are the low-fat and low-cholesterol foods?" the old man asked timidly. Peter lectured, "That's the best part...you can eat as much as you like, of whatever you like, and you never get fat, and you never get sick. This is heaven."

With that the old man went into a fit of anger, throwing down his hat, stomping on it, and shrieking wildly. Peter and his wife both tried to calm him down, asking him what was wrong. The old man looked at his wife and said, "This is all your fault. If it weren't for your blasted bran muffins, I could have been here ten years ago!"

All humor aside, you might argue with what I believe, but please don't disagree with what God's Word says. You can have more of the Lord's provision than what you are currently living on.

A few years ago, I was invited to be the guest speaker in a series of services in Ferriday, Louisiana. My wife, Rachel, came with me, as well as two other pastors and their wives, to assist me. While we were there, a very gracious woman made arrangements for us to stay at the Monmouth Plantation, which is across the Mississippi River in Natchez, Mississippi. The Monmouth Plantation is an antebellum plantation home from the Civil War era and has been the movie set of several motion pictures. This luxurious home has been listed as one of the top 100 lodging accommodations in the United States and one of the top 500 in the world. We were all amazed how the Lord provided, having made it possible for all of us to stay two nights in this luxurious place.

During the trip, the church where we were ministering had promised they would feed us all very well for lunch and supper each day. Normally while traveling, we would be on our own for breakfast. We all would have liked to have eaten in the dining room, but we discovered it was a little pricier than our budgets would allow. To eat there would have been the chance of a lifetime for us. The furnishings, menu, and service would have been something we would never forget. The first morning, we all simply skipped breakfast. The second morning, one of the pastors went to town and purchased half a dozen donuts to be shared among the six of us.

As we were preparing to leave, the manager came to visit with us. She asked, "Did you enjoy your stay? Were the beds comfortable? Did you walk the gardens and around the lake?" She then asked us a question, and we did not know exactly what to reply. I was the one doing the speaking in the nightly services, so the others naturally looked to me for my response. The question she asked was, "How was the breakfast?" I am sure I stuttered before I finally found the right words. I said, "We were very blessed to have stayed here, but honestly we looked at the menu and decided breakfast was a little more expensive than we felt we were able to pay."

The manager quickly took a step back and exclaimed, "Couldn't afford?" She then asked, "Didn't the maitre d' tell you that breakfast was included with the room?" To which I replied, "No, he didn't." Then she asked, "Didn't you read on the message beside the telephone that breakfast was included?" I responded, "No, we didn't."

People often say, "A preacher can make a good message from anything." I was not about to miss the opportunity to make a message out of this humorous event. We often do not tell people what Christ has made available for everyone. Christians are not telling others the good news that Jesus not only saves, but He also heals. On the other hand, even if Christians are to blame for not sharing the message, the Bible is readily available in every motel room, and Christian radio and television programs are being broadcast twenty-four hours a day. Ultimately every person has access to the message of hope and healing, and they cannot blame others for not telling them.

Since the fall of man, God has provided an opportunity for salvation and healing. When approached by Satan, Eve's initial reaction to his words, which began man's fall, was to doubt that God meant what He had said. Unfortunately, when we doubt God's Word, we also doubt God's cure.

Doubting God's cure and living in unbelief did not begin in our day. Unbelief was prevalent in Jesus' day too, and it is also found in the Old Testament. Although King Asa was a godly king, when he was confronted with sickness, he found it easier to trust in the physicians than to trust in God.

> *And Asa in the thirty and ninth year of his reign was diseased in his feet, until his disease was exceeding great: yet in his disease he sought not to the Lord, but to the physicians. And Asa slept with his fathers, and died in the one and fortieth year of his reign. And they buried him in his own sepulchres, which he had made for himself* (2 Chronicles 16:12–14).

When it was obvious the physicians were not able to help, he still didn't trust God. He gave orders to have a tomb prepared for himself. Since he was diseased in his feet, it could be said that he did not have a leg to stand on. The end of the story is not a happy one. He soon died and they buried him in his tomb. In essence, when people refuse to look to God's cure, they have dug their own graves.

> *It is better to trust in the Lord than to put confidence in man* (Psalm 118:8).

Too many people let their opinions, pride, or inaccurate doctrine lead to their demise. People often refuse to trust God for their healing, and then they question why God does not do something about their predicament.

I have a friend who absolutely refused to receive prayer for her disease. She grew up in a pastor's home where divine healing was not embraced. Even though she had overwhelming health issues, she found it easier to trust the doctors for her health and reduced God to One who would just give her daily strength. The medicine prescribed for her did as much harm to her body as the actual illness. One day when the pain became unbearable, I overheard her asking friends to pray that "God would give someone the knowledge to produce a new medicine to help me." My thought was, *Why not simply trust God to heal, rather than believe He could give a man a formula for a new medicine to help her deal with the pain?*

Doctors can be very helpful, but I always tell people, "Trust God for your miracle, and if nothing else happens, go to the doctor." Jesus was sent to earth to demonstrate the Father's love. Jesus was moved with compassion, and He always met people's needs.

Jesus went forth, and saw a great multitude, and was moved with compassion toward them, and he healed their sick (Matthew 14:14).

Jesus realized there were more needs than any one person could address, so He commissioned His disciples to go out and do the same.

Into whatsoever city ye enter…heal the sick that are therein, and say unto them, The kingdom of God is come nigh unto you (Luke 10:8–9).

And he said unto them, Go ye into all the world, and preach the gospel to every creature. He that believeth and is baptized shall be saved; but he that believeth not shall be damned. And these signs shall follow them that believe; In my name shall they cast out devils; they shall speak with new tongues; They shall take up serpents; and if they drink any deadly thing, it shall not hurt them; they shall lay hands on the sick, and they shall recover. So then after the Lord had spoken unto them, he was received up into heaven, and sat on the right hand of God. And they went forth, and preached every where, the Lord working with them, and confirming the word with signs following. Amen (Mark 16:15–20).

On one of my ministry trips to Ireland, I was speaking at a church in Clonmel. Because the pastor's wife was a registered nurse, she had a lot of influence in the medical community, and many health care professionals attended the church. For this particular Sunday morning service, the Lord impressed upon me to conduct a healing service. This was not unusual, but what made this difficult was the fact that there were three doctors and five RNs in attendance.

My experience has taught me that even though doctors may be Spirit-filled, they often have a very difficult time believing God for miracles. For this service, the thought of being under the scrutiny of medical professionals made me nervous.

As the service progressed and miracles began to happen, I felt the Holy Spirit prompt me to bring these doctors up to the front and show them how they could lay hands on the sick themselves. As I did this and gave the doctors "orders" to place their hand here or there and then repeat after me, the miracles that had been flowing through me began to flow through them. I visited Clonmel again a few years later, and one of the doctors told me that his own child, on whom he had laid hands and for whom he believed God for a miracle in that service, had been healed.

Back in Texas, during a service, I called a man out of the congregation because I was convinced that God wanted to heal him. I knew he was a skeptic, but I thought, *When God heals him, he will believe.* He came forward, and several people gathered around me to believe God with me for his healing. I noticed the man crossed his arms as I began to minister—not a good sign if there is any truth to body language. Absolutely nothing happened. I couldn't believe it! I questioned my heart as to how I had missed God. The next night during the testimony service, a little woman came up all excited and wanted to testify of her healing the night before. I thought this was strange because she did not even come up for prayer. She testified that when we prayed for "that man"—and she pointed her finger at the one from the night before— she said, "I had the same problem he had, but when you prayed for him, I got healed." It was obvious there was a healing to be received, but the one it was intended for was not healed because of unbelief.

I have had people stop me as I began to pray for them and tell me it was not important to them to be healed. When someone does receive their healing, they could be confronted with integrity issues. If someone is, in fact, healed, it could be considered dishonest and even fraudulent, if they continue to receive a monthly check for their disability or illness that no longer exists.

Humorously, I must admit, people have come to prayer lines and asked God for their healing. After petitioning for healing, they then ask to be remembered in prayer for an upcoming disability hearing, for favor with the judge. In that situation, I always think, *You can't have it both ways!* No wonder some people are not healed. They are unwilling to give up their disability checks.

Don't be disappointed if a prayer is not completely answered immediately. In Ireland, two ministers who were with me were called to a hospital to pray over a woman who was in the final stages of pancreatic cancer. Her husband had turned to God for help because the doctors could do nothing more for his wife, and they were desperate. He had seen an invitation to our healing services in the local paper and was convinced God could heal and decided he had nothing to lose.

As we entered the room and began to pray, the nurses didn't appear too impressed, and they suddenly decided it was time to have a CAT scan taken. I never understood why, if the woman was dying, the procedure had to be done in the first place—and especially right at that moment. We were not fully satisfied with the amount of time we were able to minister to her, but all we could do was trust God.

Two weeks after I arrived home, I received a glowing report. According to the CAT scan, the cancer had shrunk to half the size that it had been. I thought to myself, *That is good news, but I know God could have done better than that.* Although she and her husband were thankful, I was puzzled as to why she received only half of the miracle they were expecting. A couple of weeks later, I received the rest of the testimony that I had expected all along. A new CAT scan confirmed that the pancreatic cancer was completely gone. I then understood what had happened. The technician had taken the scan while the miracle was happening. If they had waited just a few more moments, the cancer would have completely disappeared. The tumor was shrinking as the first scan was being taken.

When God does, in fact, give you your miracle, do not let anyone, not even a doctor, make you doubt it ever happened. Most people I know who have received a miracle have had to fight to keep it. You may have to often remind the devil to leave you alone and refuse to allow the sickness or disease to come back.

While I was preaching in South Texas, a woman came forward on a Sunday morning for prayer after she saw miracles begin to happen. She said she had suffered with severe back problems for years and was scheduled for surgery the following Thursday. When prayer was offered on her behalf, she was instantly healed. She bent over, touched her toes, jumped, twisted, and danced—doing all the things she had not been able to do for many years.

She kept her doctor's appointment that had been scheduled for Wednesday, which was to prepare her for surgery. She testified to the doctor that her back gave her no pain, and she could do things she had not been able to do in years. I would like to tell you that the doctor was completely amazed, and that he celebrated with her, but it was quite the opposite.

The doctor explained to her that, because she had suffered for years, her surgery was scheduled for the next morning, and since the insurance company was covering her injury, she should go ahead and have the procedure. In his view she needed to make sure her problem was taken care of. Because she trusted the recommendation of the doctor more than the report of the Lord, her surgery did not go as planned. The doctor made mistakes and now the lady has a condition with her back that is far worse than it was before she received prayer.

If you truly believe God's Word, you will have the faith needed to believe God's cure for whatever sickness or disease you struggle with.

Who hath believed our report? and to whom is the arm of the Lord revealed? (Isaiah 53:1)

Chapter Thirteen

Not Your Usual Miracles

They were all amazed, and glorified God, saying, We never saw it on this fashion (Mark 2:12).

Anyone who has ever believed in divine healing has had someone disagree with them about their faith. The skeptic would say, "I just don't believe a man can put his hands on someone and heal them." I have heard this argument many times; each time I hear it, the one defending their unbelieving position would always think they have me hemmed into a corner. To be completely honest, I believe the same way. If you don't have faith, your touch is just that—a touch. But if you do have faith, a touch can change everything.

And these signs shall follow them that believe; In my name shall they cast out devils; they shall speak with new tongues; They shall take up serpents; and if they drink any deadly thing, it shall not hurt them; they shall lay hands on the sick, and they shall recover (Mark 16:17–18).

In my experience, the ones who do not believe in laying hands on the sick often say they follow the other scriptural command, which is found in the book of James:

Is any among you afflicted? let him pray.... Is any sick among you? let him call for the elders of the church; and let them pray over him, anointing him with oil in the name of the Lord: And the prayer of faith shall save the sick, and the Lord shall raise him up (James 5:13–15).

The first command we see in this passage from James is that the one who is afflicted should pray for himself. My phone often rings from people asking for prayer. I do not mind coming into agreement with them, but I must say I am not paid to pray so that they don't have to. I find myself being as concerned about people's situations as they are themselves.

If someone follows this example and it doesn't appear to work, he should then call the elders of the church and be anointed with oil in the name of the Lord. Prayers made in faith will be answered. But let me ask, "How are the elders anointing with oil?" Doesn't anointing with oil involve touching or the laying on of hands? People follow this example because James, the half brother of our Lord, commanded it, but they won't do what Jesus Himself said to do by the laying on of hands. Why put faith in the words of James rather than the words of Jesus?

In a typical, Spirit-filled healing service, people who desire prayer are lined up across the front of the church. As music is played from the Hammond organ, the pastor and the church elders minister to those who have come forward, anointing them with oil and praying. This is the way that the early disciples did it...or is it? This method is certainly not one that Jesus used.

The gifts of God, which operate in each of us, may vary as much as our personalities. People often challenge you when the way you operate in your gift is different from what they have done or have seen others do. Though the operation may be different, the Source is the same. There is usually not a right or wrong way of administering the gift. The difference is, as the Spirit flows through us, our personalities come into play, which in itself is not necessarily a bad thing.

Now there are diversities of gifts, but the same Spirit. And there are dif-ferences of administrations, but the same Lord. And there are diversities of operations, but it is the same God which worketh all in all (1 Corinthians 12:4–6).

If divine healing presents a challenge to you, I must caution you that what I am about to share may offend your opinions. My observations are not meant to be divisive. I encourage you to examine the scriptures for yourself and decide whether or not we are interpreting the healing ministry of Jesus accurately. The way Jesus conducted His personal ministry is a pattern for us. What better example to follow than His?

While I am not against anointing with oil, it was never recorded that Jesus did this. According to Scripture, the disciples only did it once: the first time Jesus sent them forth in ministry, and this was before they were filled with the Spirit in the Upper Room.

> *And they cast out many devils, and anointed with oil many that were sick, and healed them* (Mark 6:13).

I am not against praying for the sick, but it is never recorded that Jesus, or His disciples, did this either. In John 21:25, the apostle stated that "even the world itself could not contain the books that should be written of Jesus, of all that Jesus said and did." Something as important as prayer for the sick or Jesus' anointing with oil, however, would certainly have been documented in the four gospels if it were required procedure for us in our ministry. It is easy to assume the way Jesus ministered to the sick is the way He also intended for us to do it, as well.

> *...as my Father hath sent me, even so send I you* (John 20:21).

I am not suggesting that we do not pray for the sick. An anointing to heal the sick comes through our times of quietness and solitude with our heavenly Father. The disciples learned this principle of prayer early in their ministry. Once you have prayed, then go and do all Christ has instructed. If we do not transition from the prayer meeting to obedience, we have made all of our praying ineffective.

> *But thou, when thou prayest, enter into thy closet, and when thou hast shut thy door, pray to thy Father which is in secret; and thy Father which seeth in secret shall reward thee openly* (Matthew 6:6).

Through intimate time with the Father, the same Spirit that Christ Himself was filled with has been placed within us.

> *Then said Jesus to them again, Peace be unto you: as my Father hath sent*

me, even so send I you. And when he had said this, he breathed on them, and saith unto them, Receive ye the Holy Ghost (John 20:21–22).

He that believeth on me, the works that I do shall he do also; and greater works than these shall he do; because I go unto my Father. And whatsoever ye shall ask in my name, that will I do, that the Father may be glorified in the Son. If ye shall ask any thing in my name, I will do it (John 14:12–14).

If ye abide in me, and my words abide in you, ye shall ask what ye will, and it shall be done unto you (John 15:7).

Do not bring the All-Powerful, Eternal Christ down to your level of thinking. While Moses was on the mountain hearing from God, the unbelieving Israelites who had stubbornly refused to make the journey up the mountain with him, had reduced God to a golden calf, saying, "These be thy gods, O Israel, which brought thee up out of the land of Egypt" (Exodus 32:4). Before God could move in my life, even though I had been raised in a spiritual culture of the supernatural, I had to unlearn as much as I had to learn about the nature and heart of Christ.

A common remark people make when they argue against divine healing is, "If it were true, why not go to the hospital and heal everyone?" Any person who has a gifting in this area will tell you that it doesn't work that way. Although Jesus did not heal all who were sick, He did heal all who came to Him and asked. Not every sick person has faith and is willing to believe for their healing.

Jesus did not anoint with oil, and He did not pray for the sick. So, how did He heal? The Gospels are full of examples of the many methods He used.

He sent His word:

And when Jesus was entered into Capernaum, there came unto him a centurion, beseeching him, And saying, Lord, my servant lieth at home sick of the palsy, grievously tormented. And Jesus saith unto him, I will come and heal him. The centurion answered and said, Lord, I am not worthy that thou shouldest come under my roof: but speak the word only, and my servant shall be healed. For I am a man under authority, having soldiers under me: and I say to this man, Go, and he goeth; and to another, Come, and he cometh; and to my servant, Do this, and he doeth it. When Jesus heard it, he marvelled, and said to them that followed, Verily I say unto you, I have not found so great faith, no, not in Israel... And Jesus said unto the centurion, Go thy way; and as thou hast believed, so be it done unto thee. And his servant was healed in the selfsame hour (Matthew 8:5–10, 13).

He spit:

And he cometh to Bethsaida; and they bring a blind man unto him, and besought him to touch him. And he took the blind man by the hand, and led him out of the town; and when he had spit on his eyes, and put his hands upon him, he asked him if he saw ought. And he looked up, and said, I see men as trees, walking. After that he put his hands again upon his eyes, and made him look up: and he was restored, and saw every man clearly (Mark 8:22–25).

He spit, put His fingers in their ears, and touched their tongues:

And they bring unto him one that was deaf, and had an impediment in his speech; and they beseech him to put his hand upon him. And he took him aside from the multitude, and put his fingers into his ears, and he spit, and touched his tongue; And looking up to heaven, he sighed, and saith unto him, Ephphatha, that is, Be opened. And straightway his ears were opened, and the string of his tongue was loosed, and he spake plain (Mark 7:32–35).

He laid His hands on people:

Now when the sun was setting, all they that had any sick with divers diseases brought them unto him; and he laid his hands on every one of them, and healed them (Luke 4:40).

He honored an act of obedience:

And they come unto him, bringing one sick of the palsy, which was borne of four. And when they could not come nigh unto him for the press, they uncovered the roof where he was: and when they had broken it up, they let down the bed wherein the sick of the palsy lay. When Jesus saw their faith he said unto the sick of the palsy, Son, thy sins be forgiven thee…, I say unto thee, Arise, and take up thy bed, and go thy way into thine house. And immediately he arose, took up the bed, and went forth before them all; insomuch that they were all amazed, and glorified God, saying, We never saw it on this fashion (Mark 2:3–5, 11–12).

People touched Him:

And when they were gone over, they came into the land of Gennesaret. And when the men of that place had knowledge of him, they sent out into all that country round about, and brought unto him all that were diseased; And besought him that they might only touch the hem of his garment: and as many as touched were made perfectly whole *(Matthew 14:34–36).*

He rewarded personal faith:

And they came to Jericho: and as he went out of Jericho with his disciples and a great number of people, blind Bartimaeus, the son of Timaeus, sat by the highway side begging. And when he heard that it was Jesus of Nazareth, he began to cry out, and say, Jesus, thou Son of David, have mercy on me. And many charged him that he should hold his peace: but he cried the more a great deal, Thou Son of David, have mercy on me. And Jesus stood still, and commanded him to be called. And they call the blind man, saying unto him, Be of good comfort, rise; he calleth thee. And he, casting away his garment, rose, and came to Jesus. And Jesus answered and said unto him, What wilt thou that I should do unto thee? The blind man said unto him, Lord, that I might receive my sight. And Jesus said unto him, Go thy way; thy faith hath made thee whole. And immediately he received his sight, and followed Jesus in the way (Mark 10:46–52).

Two other methods that Jesus used involve an entirely different subject. When someone is sick as the result of an unclean spirit, before they can be cured from the disease or illness, the evil spirit must be driven out. One word of caution: before their deliverance, be sure the person receiving ministry desires to be set free and be certain they are willing to do whatever it takes to remain free. If someone is not committed to their deliverance, the spirits will come back and bring others with them. In Matthew 12 we are told that when an unclean spirit leaves, it will attempt to return if the house is empty. It will also bring seven other spirits more wicked than itself, and the last state of the individual will be worse than the first.

He rebuked evil spirits:

And when they were come to the multitude, there came to him a certain man, kneeling down to him, and saying, Lord, have mercy on my son: for he is lunatick, and sore vexed: for ofttimes he falleth into the fire, and oft into the water. And I brought him to thy disciples, and they could not cure him. Then Jesus answered and said, O faithless and perverse generation, how long shall I be with you? how long shall I suffer you? bring him hither to me. And Jesus rebuked the devil; and he departed out of him: and the child was cured from that very hour (Matthew 17:14–18).

He cast out devils:

When the even was come, they brought unto him many that were possessed with devils: and he cast out the spirits with his word, and healed all that were sick (Matthew 8:16).

It is very fitting after Jesus healed the man of palsy, who was let down through the roof by his friends, the people had an unusual response: "They were all amazed, and glorified God, saying, We never saw it on this fashion" (Mark 2:12).

The early church took miracles to an entirely new level. Just as Jesus saved the best wine for last at the wedding in Cana, I also believe the last-days church can declare, "The best is yet to come!" As the anointing flows from believers, one or more gifts come into action, making healing available to hurting people, and miracles happen.

For to one is given by the Spirit the word of wisdom; to another the word of knowledge by the same Spirit; to another faith by the same Spirit; to another the gifts of healing by the same Spirit; to another the working of miracles; to another prophecy; to another discerning of spirits (1 Corinthians 12:8–10).

A person could argue, "If Christ is the sole provider, then why does healing come through a man?" Couldn't the same be said about the preaching of the Gospel? Christ is the sole provider of salvation, yet God brings the message of salvation through men.

For whosoever shall call upon the name of the Lord shall be saved. How then shall they call on him in whom they have not believed? and how shall they believe in him of whom they have not heard? and how shall they hear without a preacher? (Romans 10:13–14).

There is much more to receiving a miracle than "just receiving a miracle." Some people talk about faith, and they think because they have some form of it, they will receive from God. There is a huge difference between having faith in God and having faith in faith. Even demons have faith: "the devils also believe, and tremble" (James 2:9). Receiving a miracle is about faith in Christ and His atoning blood, which has been appropriated for you. Yes, healing is available to everyone.

Christ told the disciples, "And as ye go, preach, saying, The kingdom of heaven is at hand. Heal the sick, cleanse the lepers, raise the dead, cast out devils: freely ye have received, freely give" (Matthew 10:7–8).

In my opinion, miracles should be placed into two categories. The first should include "regular miracles," and the second, "special miracles." If a person has difficulty believing in "regular miracles," then the "special miracles" are going to challenge him.

A "regular miracle" can be orchestrated, as James stated, by calling for the elders of the church and anointing with oil. Paul's ministry, much like Jesus', included things that went beyond explanation. These would be considered "special miracles."

And God wrought special miracles by the hands of Paul: So that from his body were brought unto the sick handkerchiefs or aprons, and the diseases departed from them, and the evil spirits went out of them (Acts 19:11–12).

In concluding this chapter, I want to share a few "special miracles" with you. These are accounts of how I have seen God move in amazing ways. Some have no explanation other than the fact that God is good. Remember, "Your Father knoweth what things ye have need of, before ye ask him" (Matthew 6:8). One does not need another believer to bring healing; faith in God is simple enough. There are occasions, though, when God uses a man to stir up faith or open a door into the supernatural.

Many years ago, a man from Corrigan had been seriously injured in an automobile accident on a Saturday evening. Because of his condition, he had been taken by a medical helicopter to a hospital in Houston, a couple of hours away. He was placed on life support and was in a comatose state. I was called to a local hospital with his other family members who had been injured along with his wife, who had received a shattered knee (which God instantly healed). Because of my ministry to his family and my church obligations on Sunday morning, I could not go to the hospital until that evening. The man in the accident had a sister-in-law who attended my church who informed the rest of her family, "Everything will be all right when Brother Phil gets here." I was not aware of what she had told them, but as my wife and I walked into the ICU waiting room and talked to the family, the nurse came running out of the unit and with excitement in her voice told his wife, "Your husband just came out of the coma." (At the time, I did not know, but we were on the opposite side of the wall from where the man lay.) He was healed, but I do not know if it was because of what I was sent there to do and the authority it carried, or if it was because of the faith of a family member who believed.

The story is told in the Book of Acts of the shadow of Peter falling on the sick and they were healed. A Spirit-filled believer has the ability to change the atmosphere with just his or her presence. Walking in the anointing can be compared to one who opens a door into the supernatural where miracles easily happen. Just their presence, their touch, or their word brings life and hope. May I remind you that the Holy Spirit lives inside of us.

The following is a personal testimony that occurred because I opened a door into the supernatural realm right in my own living room. This woman's faith connected with God, who was able to change her situation.

I was the RN director of a cardiovascular center, and I worked a very busy pace. I was rounding a corner one day and fell. At the emergency room, I was diagnosed with a broken bone in my knee. I was leaving that weekend for a visit to Corrigan, Texas, to see Pastor Phil and Rachel, and attend church. Because of the upcoming trip, I did not allow a cast to be put on; instead I was given a brace. The orthopedic doctor gave me instructions to return Monday for casting. I told him that where I was going was special, and I'd be healed by Monday. He said, "There is no way God will heal you, and on Monday, I'll take another X-ray myself."

We got to Pastor Phil's house and he noticed me limping. I told him that I had broken my knee—a definitive diagnosis by an orthopedic physician. Pastor Phil said, "Why don't we do something about that right now?" Because I am an RN, I am totally skeptical about healings, but I love Jesus and know that anything could be possible. Pastor Phil said, "I believe God has already done it," and the swelling started going down and I could walk on my knee without pain. The following day I attended Sunday church without my brace or crutches and was PAIN FREE... I went to the doctor's office on Monday and literally skipped in. The orthopedist was dumbfounded. He could not figure out what had happened. He took an X-ray and there was no more fracture. He said "There must be a mix-up with the X-rays. There is no way the X-ray with the fracture was yours." But I knew otherwise. —*Eileen Turner, Mamou, Louisiana*

In a church service in Gonzales, Texas, a woman came forward because of a protruding hernia, the size of a grapefruit. Her husband, though he was an unbeliever, came with her, so I had him lay his hand on her abdomen over the protrusion. I did not pray. I just spoke to the hernia and commanded it to go back into the lining of the abdomen. The hernia immediately shrank, and her husband felt it when it happened. For the first time in years, she was able to look straight down and see her feet. This all happened when a preacher only spoke to her condition and an unbelieving husband laid hands on his wife.

In Ireland, a Catholic woman came forward for ministry. She had a twisted arm that had grown into an unnatural position as the result of an injury. Though this was not the way she believed, she had heard miracles were happening and figured she had nothing to lose. As I ministered during the healing flow, she stood up in front of everyone and wanted me to do something about her arm. Personally I felt helpless, but with Jesus, all things are possible. I simply closed my eyes and grabbed her arm. I can't even remember what I said because the moment I started speaking, her arm began untwisting, and the joints loosened, until she had full range of motion. Her daughter later testified she had been in an accident, and because of inadequate medical care, her arm had not healed properly. She had not been able to comb her hair or touch her face with that hand in over four years.

I was called to Baytown, Texas, to pray for a lady with a serious heart condition in a hospital. As I ministered to this woman, I turned to her son, touched his arm, and said, "Lord, meet his need, whatever it is." I did not know he had a severe skin disorder beneath his clothes that left his skin scaly. He called me later that day and told me that just a few minutes after I left the room, he went to the restroom and discovered his skin was as smooth as a baby's. He took off his clothes and shook them out, removing the dead skin.

I was invited to conduct a healing service in San Antonio, Texas. Johnny Knight, the pastor who often travels with me, gave the youth pastor and his wife there a very encouraging word. The couple came for prayer because the wife needed a healing in the abdomen. Johnny was not aware that she'd experienced several miscarriages over the past year, and the most recent was only just weeks earlier.

Rather than pray, Johnny looked at the young lady and told her to "Mark your calendar, because by this day the next year, you will hold a baby in your arms." The young wife went home and marked her calendar as she had been instructed to do.

A few months passed and I received an e-mail from her, and she told me she had just come from the doctor's office, and she was again pregnant. The doctor projected her due date to be exactly one year from the day the word was given.

The pastor contacted me and requested that Johnny and I return on the date, one year later, and conduct another healing service. When we arrived in San Antonio the day before the service, the baby had not yet been born. We had no doubt, because we believe the word of the Lord, that the baby would be born before the service the next morning. As we sat with the pastor eating supper, he received a call that the youth pastor and his wife were at the hospital, and she was going into labor. Before we finished eating, the baby was born. Although she was not able to attend the service, a picture was shown during the service of the new mother holding the baby in her arms—exactly one year from the date the prophecy was given!

When will we understand and believe? God uses people to administer healing. God is able to heal without the use of our hands. He can also use words, commands, thoughts, and actions. Let us remember it is He who does the work; we are only vessels in which the supernatural God can flow through.

Now unto him that is able to do exceeding abundantly above all that we ask or think, according to the power that worketh in us (Ephesians 3:20).

Amazing things will happen when we yield ourselves to the Holy Spirit. Maybe miracles have not happened in your life or maybe not as frequently as you would like. Let's turn loose of ideas and myths of ministry and fully believe God for the miraculous. It can happen, if you catch your second wind.

Chapter Fourteen

God's Favorite Recipe

*And thou shalt make it an oil of holy ointment, an ointment compound
after the art of the apothecary: it shall be an holy anointing oil* (Exodus
30:25).

While the children of Israel wandered in the desert for forty years,
God gave Moses the instructions for constructing the tabernacle, the
furnishings, and the tapestries. Everything had to be built precisely the
way God told him. Once the construction was completed, God gave
Aaron the list of ingredients to produce the holy anointing oil.
Everything in the tabernacle, every piece of furniture, as well as all of
the priests, were required to be anointed with this oil.

*Moreover the Lord spake unto Moses, saying, Take thou also unto thee
principal spices, of pure myrrh five hundred shekels, and of sweet cinnamon half so much, even two hundred and fifty shekels, and of sweet
calamus two hundred and fifty shekels, And of cassia five hundred
shekels, after the shekel of the sanctuary, and of oil olive an hin: And
thou shalt make it an oil of holy ointment, an ointment compound after
the art of the apothecary: it shall be an holy anointing oil* (Exodus
30:22–25).

The instructions for the oil were actually a list of ingredients with
instructions for mixing what could be referred to as a recipe. Let me re-
word and rearrange this Scripture in such a way that it may be a little

more understandable. If this were found in a woman's kitchen, this might be what the recipe card would have looked like.

Recipe for Holy Anointing Oil

Take the following fine spices:
12 pounds of MYRRH
6 pounds of CINNAMON
6 pounds of CALAMUS
12 pounds of CASSIA
4 quarts of OLIVE OIL
Blend these into the holy anointing oil, a fragrant blend, the work of a perfumer. It will be the sacred anointing oil. (See Exodus 30:23.)

These were not just random ingredients or spices that God chose for the taste or the smell. Each of these ingredients represented something specific He was looking for. I want to break down the ingredients and share with you what I believe God is looking for in believers who are determined to walk in a greater anointing.

As my congregation and I were preparing for what we sensed God was about to do in our lives, I shared this message. Once revival came to our church, I again shared it because I knew what we did to prepare ourselves was the same thing we would do to maintain what God was doing.

12 pounds of pure MYRRH

Myrrh is a small, thorny bush that grows in arid country on stony ground. When the bush is "wounded," it produces a gummy resin, which has a sweet smell but a very bitter taste.

Myrrh represents a life of selflessness and servitude. Like the gummy resin that does not flow freely, putting our own desires aside and taking up a higher cause is not usually a desirable task. Serving others sometimes leaves a bitter taste in our mouths, but it is a sweet smell in the nostrils of God.

Service is a lost art. God requires this quality in those whom He trusts with the anointing because we are not called to serve our own desires. Jesus told His disciples in Matthew 6:25: "Take no thought for your life." God is going to use men who are willing to lay their lives down for the Kingdom.

But seek ye first the kingdom of God, and his righteousness; and all these things shall be added unto you (Matthew 6:33).

A very important principle that guides my life while serving others is this: What you make happen for others, God will make happen for you.

And the Lord turned the captivity of Job, when he prayed for his friends: also the Lord gave Job twice as much as he had before (Job 42:10).

Egyptians often used myrrh for embalming. The things we do for Christ and others will have eternal value. When the woman came and anointed Jesus' feet, He said it would be mentioned wherever the Gospel was preached as a memorial to her.

Wheresoever this gospel shall be preached throughout the whole world, this also that she hath done shall be spoken of for a memorial of her (Mark 14:9).

6 pounds of sweet CINNAMON

Cinnamon comes from the bark of a tree, and it literally means "to be upright," or what we refer to in Christian circles as holiness. The bark is very sweet, but the branches produce a flower with a pungent aroma; when it is in bloom, the air can become putrid, making it very difficult to breathe.

Cinnamon was used by God to remind us that it is necessary to walk upright, to live holy, and to remain sweet, although everything around us may stink. It is the sweetness that counters the stench of the blossom much the same way a Christian is expected to impact the world around them.

The one who walks with God must walk in integrity and holiness before Him. We are called to shine as a light in a dark place. Even though we are surrounded by sin, it must not influence us.

Be blameless and harmless, the sons of God, without rebuke, in the midst of a crooked and perverse nation, among whom ye shine as lights in the world (Philippians 2:15).

6 pounds of sweet CALAMUS

Calamus is neither sweet nor aromatic. It is a grass that grows on the bottom of a swamp or marsh and thrives in what appears to be an environment where little else can live. It survives because it has the ability to produce shoots, or long blades of hollow grass much like straws that can reach the surface of the water. The blades of grass draw oxygen from "another world" and bring it down to where it is needed. The word calamus literally means "a rod of strength when challenged."

Many times you have to stand alone in a difficult place. The enemy doesn't think you will be able to make it there, but because you are trusting God, you can actually flourish. You can't quit because you get weary. Though your flesh wants to crumble, you will remain faithful where you have been placed.

Be ye stedfast, unmoveable, always abounding in the work of the Lord, forasmuch as ye know that your labour is not in vain in the Lord (1 Corinthians 15:58).

When you are able to thrive, you actually bring life and hope to others around you. That rough spot you are in may be a place where others have failed. Never give up. We are of no benefit to the Kingdom if we abort our mission. Oftentimes the calling on our lives will leave us feeling overwhelmed. If God has called you to where you are, you can rest assured that you are never alone. Victory is established in your heart before it is made manifest on the battlefield. You need to change your mind-set from surviving to thriving.

12 pounds of CASSIA

Cassia is found in the bark of a small bush that has neither taste nor smell. It is included in the recipe, not for what it adds to the mixture but for what it represents. Cassia produces a small purple flower and is only found in high altitudes.

Though it will usually be unnoticed and unrecognized, the color of its flower is purple, which represents royalty or something fitting for a king. He uses us to do something for Him, but we cannot let what we do cause us to become arrogant. There is no glory for ourselves in what we do. That is the reason this small flower was chosen. God cannot use us if we become self-promoting. Everything we do is by Him, about Him, and for Him. We must walk humbly before God, never bringing attention to ourselves and never claiming God's glory as our own.

I am the Lord: that is my name: and my glory will I not give to another (Isaiah 42:8).

Herod, the ruler of Galilee arrayed in his kingly apparel, made a speech, and people praised him as if he were a god. The angel of the Lord smote him, and he was eaten up by worms in front of the people because he did not give God the glory.

And upon a set day Herod, arrayed in royal apparel, sat upon his throne, and made an oration unto them. And the people gave a shout, saying, It is the voice of a god, and not of a man. And immediately the angel of the Lord smote him, because he gave not God the glory: and he was eaten of worms, and gave up the ghost (Acts 12:21–23).

Pride is a major pitfall to be avoided at all costs. When God promotes us, it is often tempting to think we are "more than we really are." May I remind you, that miracle you just shared didn't come from you; that healing was not from your hand; the prophetic word you delivered was not from your heart. Remember, God uses everyone, and what you have accomplished for Him was never meant to lift you up. Solomon said, "Pride goes before destruction and a haughty spirit before a fall."

When God sees you can be trusted, He will give you more responsibility or authority. Remember, you can lose something as quickly as you gained it. In the words of Job, "The Lord gives and the Lord takes away…"

4 quarts of OLIVE OIL

Olive oil is the only fluid component in the recipe. Oil unifies, blends, or brings together all the other ingredients to make the mixture complete. Those who make it their aim to build the Kingdom will find their anointing increasing. You can be the one who brings people together when all they have ever known is bitterness and confusion. Love, like oil, makes everything go much more smoothly.

> *Behold, how good and how pleasant it is for brethren to dwell together in unity! It is like the precious ointment upon the head, that ran down upon the beard, even Aaron's beard: that went down to the skirts of his garments; As the dew of Hermon, and as the dew that descended upon the mountains of Zion: for there the Lord commanded the blessing, even life for evermore* (Psalm 133:1–3).

In some churches and Christian circles, ministry can be competitive. We must remember that we are not building our own kingdom. Jesus gave us the example in the Lord's Prayer: "For thine is the kingdom, and the power, and the glory, for ever" (Matthew 6:13). And when He said amen, that settled it.

The Body of Christ's greatest enemy does not come from without, but from within. We are often guilty of attacking ourselves. In the medical world, when blood cells fight other cells, it is called cancer. I can only imagine what would happen if we started uplifting, encouraging, and praying for one another—even those outside our "interpretation of Scripture," or "circle of friends."

No matter how accurate the message you are preaching, if you are attacking others, you are damaging the Body. On the one hand, you can preach the cross and the blood of Jesus; but if on the other hand, you are tearing down the Body, what good are you really accomplishing?

The sign that we truly have the love of Christ is when we can love others, even though their views theologically, politically, or socially are different from ours. If Jesus can sit and eat at a table with a sinner, can we not sit and fellowship one with another? I am not referring to those who are in blatant sin and have lifestyles contrary to the Word of God; to such, the Scriptures tell us to avoid fellowship, and not to call such people brothers. But what would happen if we realized that we are all on the same team and found a way to work together?

I have listed the five ingredients that are necessary in the recipe for the holy anointing oil. There is one more aspect to this formula which is important to understand and this is the quantities of each of the elements in the mixture. Once again, I re-word this in such a way as to easily understand their importance.

12 pounds of MYRRH
6 pounds of CINNAMON
6 pounds of CALAMUS
12 pounds of CASSIA
4 quarts of OLIVE OIL

Of the dry ingredients, twice as much myrrh and cassia were required as cinnamon and calamus. Myrrh represents serving others, and cassia represents giving God glory. Cinnamon represents holiness, and calamus represents stability. What this tells us is that God expects all these attributes to be present in our lives, but it is more important to serve others, while giving Him glory, than it is to just be holy and steadfast.

God is very gracious, and He may be a little more tolerant when we slip and need to repent from time to time (cinnamon). We may occasionally get discouraged, and our walk may be a little unsteady (calamus). There is never room to think the Kingdom is about us (myrrh), or to think the things we have accomplished will promote us or make us look good (cassia). The final thing needed is a whole lot of unity (olive oil).

These are the necessary components needed in a life for God to continue to use a man. If one does not have these qualities, he will never accomplish the things the Lord expects him to do. One can do greater things for Him if he serves others and lives holy while he remains steadfast and gives God the glory. When we truly love each other and the Kingdom, these essential components are never difficult to accomplish. If you can master this recipe, you will be ready to run with your second wind.

Chapter Fifteen

Is There a Coon in Your Fig Tree?

Ye have not chosen me, but I have chosen you, and ordained you, that ye should go and bring forth fruit, and that your fruit should remain (John 15:16).

Jesus and the disciples travelled from Bethany to Jerusalem. Seeing a fig tree along the path, He became hungry. He stopped to pick some figs but was unable to find any, although the tree was covered in leaves. Jesus spoke to the tree that it would not ever bear fruit again, and it immediately dried up.

I have a large fig tree in my backyard that I had become frustrated with because year after year, I was never able to pick any figs. I tried everything I knew to do such as fertilizing and pruning it regularly. Though the tree was full of young fruit, they never reached maturity. Being fascinated with the biblical account of how Jesus dealt with fig trees that didn't produce, I was tempted to cut it down.

One night after dark, Rachel asked me to burn some household trash. (That is how you dispose of garbage when you live in the country.) I took my flashlight with me so I could see the barrel in the dark. I heard a noise in the fig tree so I flashed the light on it, and to my amazement, I saw a set of shiny little eyes, looking at me. There was a racoon in the tree eating the fruit! Raccoons are known for looking like a masked thief because of the dark patch of fur surrounding their eyes.

I knew I had to take quick action, so I borrowed a trap from a friend and began catching coons. I was amazed that when I rid myself of the

119

raccoon population, I was able to start picking large, delicious figs from my tree. Now, as I reread the story of Jesus and the fig tree, I chuckle when I think, *Did they have coons back then in Jerusalem?*

In your life, there could be things causing your tree not to produce fruit, or for the fruit not to reach maturity. The Lord is looking for fruit, not empty claims, only fruit. There is always a reason your tree is not bearing.

> *Ye have not chosen me, but I have chosen you, and ordained you, that ye should go and bring forth fruit, and that your fruit should remain* (John 15:16).

Pride, depression, unforgiveness, bad habits, addictions, lack of discipline, prejudice, laziness, lack of faith, unbelief, and many other culprits could be the reason no fruit is produced. There is nothing more frustrating than spending a lot of energy or time and having nothing to show for the trouble.

I realized two things the evening I discovered the coon in my fig tree. The first thing was that you will never be able to gather fruit from your tree if something gets to it before you do. The second thing was that God did not give a fig tree the ability to shake a coon loose from its branches. That is where the man who owns the tree comes into play. God allowed me to have a fruit tree in my yard, assuming I would protect it from anything that tried to steal its fruit. Likewise everyone needs a faithful friend who will tell them the truth concerning things in their life that attempt to steal the fruit. One also needs a pastor and a loving church family so that the good things God begins inside them will come to maturity. God did not design us to stand alone. We all need each other—and someone needs you.

To save us is exactly why God sent His Son, Jesus. We could not help ourselves. We all have the weight of sin on us because not only were we born with it, but we also have all made poor choices. Now our lives can produce fruit because He has delivered us from the things that have robbed us.

Is There a Coon in Your Fig Tree?

The Spirit of the Lord is upon me, because he hath anointed me to preach the gospel to the poor; he hath sent me to heal the brokenhearted, to preach deliverance to the captives, and recovering of sight to the blind, to set at liberty them that are bruised (Luke 4:18).

I have a special relationship with Pastor Terry LaFleur in Mamou, Louisiana. Anytime I tell him I have a word for his church, he just says, "When do you want to come and bring it?" On one such occasion, I did have a word to bring; Pastor Terry decided on a date and I could hardly wait to bring it.

During the first night of revival, I delivered this message, which I titled, "Is There a Coon in Your Fig Tree?" I knew it was not the most dynamic message I had ever preached. As I stood, I even apologized to the congregation for the simple word I was about to bring. I said, "I can preach better than this," but I knew in my heart I had heard the Holy Spirit, and I had the right message. When I minister, I am not given the option of choosing what I deliver to the people. Early in my ministry I made the decision to impact people's lives rather than impress them.

As I closed the message, I felt I should point out a young woman, call her forward, and tell her that this word was for her. I asked Kim Bourgeois to come up and told her, "If you do not get the coon out of your tree, you never will produce any fruit." Kim began to sob, and I thought to myself, *Wow! That must have been a good word.*

Kim is the daughter of Rebecca LaFleur, whose testimony I shared in chapter six. Kim and her family had recently begun attending church, and her twenty-one-year-old son, Ryan Dunn, had given his life to the Lord about three months earlier. A few weeks afterward, Ryan had suddenly died of nocturnal hypoglycemia—low blood sugar. Kim went to his room to wake him one morning and found the sight no mother ever wants to see. Her only child was dead. Ryan had been a young man full of life. He had good friends, a loving family, and a great job. Ryan was the apple of his mother's eye, and her whole world revolved around him. Now everything was shattered, and Kim did not feel like living.

Kim was having a difficult time dealing with all the emotions of losing her son. As with other mothers who had experienced the untimely death of a child, she often spent inordinate amounts of time grieving at the local cemetery. At times, Kim felt she could not handle the loss. It was only because she turned things over to the Lord, along with the loving support of her mother and family members, that she somehow found the strength to make it through each day.

When I talked to Kim the morning after I gave her that word, she told me, "You didn't know this, but Ryan had a nickname I had given him many years before. It was 'My Little Coonie,' a.k.a. 'Downtown Coonie Brown.'" She wanted to be with Ryan so badly, she often thought it would be easier to just end it all and go to be with him. But if she didn't learn to deal with these feelings, she would never be able to do what God wanted her to do to help others. This was the coon in her fig tree.

Kim has learned to submit herself to the Lord and resist the devil. Life will never again be the same for her. Even though she continues to walk with the Lord, there will always be a huge emptiness in her life. Yet in spite of her pain, she reaches out to other grieving mothers, and now her life is producing fruit. Here is an example of the fruit that God has begun producing in Kim's life, in her own words:

> After I arrived home from church on a Sunday afternoon, I decided to go shopping. Before I realized it, for some reason, I headed to Lafayette. I never like to shop there. At one point I wanted to turn around but realized I was too near to turn around and go in the opposite direction toward Alexandria. As I continued on, my alarm went off, indicating a tire was low in air pressure. I pulled in at the first gas station I could find, got out of the truck to check my tire, and I heard screams.
>
> At first, it sounded like some girls cutting up, so I listened again, but didn't hear anything. I began putting air in my tire and then heard another scream. I KNEW THAT SCREAM! I knew that scream deep in my soul because it was the scream of death...the same scream I had used myself, when I found Ryan that morning several months before...whew...this is hard to write. I immediately closed my eyes and said, "Please God...please..." and slowly stood up.
>
> When I looked around the side of my door, toward the road, I

could see a beautiful blond girl holding her arms around herself and screaming, but I didn't understand why. That was not the only scream I heard. I walked toward her...I felt like I was not walking, that it was something else, like an out-of-body experience. As I walked toward her I heard the scream again, a mother's scream...THE scream of death I knew so well.

I walked over to the little girl (about 12 to 13 years old) and wrapped my arms around her. She said, "He shook the whole car." I said, "It's going to be okay." I looked toward where she was looking and saw her mom was holding a beautiful dark-haired little boy about one and a half years of age. She had sunk to the ground as she held her baby; I knew what was wrong. I let the girl go and saw two other children standing by their mom. As the mother looked at me, I saw the despair in her eyes. I knew that look as well as I knew the scream.

I slowly walked to her and squatted down and said, "Can I pray for him?" As I stared, I remember saying, "God, YOU SAID whatever we ask is ours. I ask that You give this baby back to his mom. We are covered by the blood, and I ask in the NAME OF JESUS that You restore life and breath to this child." I don't know what else came out of my mouth, but I know I was praying. The baby's arms were blue because of a lack of oxygen. When I looked at his face, I could see Ryan's; the color was unmistakable. As I prayed, I heard another couple say they were calling 911 and asked to perform CPR. The mom had called 911 as I was praying. Then the other woman exclaimed, "Look, he's breathing...he's whimpering...he's crying!"

I slowly took my hands off of him and watched the color return from the blue ash of death to pink, as only when the blood is flowing. I stood up and looked around and wondered, *Kim, what are you doing?* I looked at the mom, and the others around, and then walked to my truck, and left. I was in shock for quite a while and all I could say was, "THANK YOU, GOD! THANK YOU, GOD!" As I was driving, I asked Him, "Why couldn't I save Ryan, my own son? Why didn't I know the words to say then?"

Later I went back to the station, and asked the clerk how the baby was. She looked at me, and said, "That baby was so blue," and I said, "I KNOW." She told me the ambulance came and they took the baby to the hospital. The baby had had an epileptic seizure, so strong it shook the whole car. The mother had been attempting CPR for over fifteen minutes to no avail. The baby did not breathe the entire time. Realizing the baby was dead, they stopped the car, and this was when I heard the screams and found the mother on the side of the road, in the grass, holding her dead baby.

Kim is turning her own tragedy into a glimmer of hope as she is sharing the loss of Ryan to bring a measure of comfort to grieving mothers. She has established a nonprofit organization, based in Mamou, called "Pathways of Hope." Land was donated and designated for a walking memorial park, a place of strength and healing for those who have experienced the untimely death of a child. Family and friends can come here and grieve, or just share memories.

Kim has taken an experience that, at times, still attempts to overwhelm her and has begun reaching out to others. It would be nice if this were someone else's story, but it is not. Please do not tell her she has a great testimony, or that you enjoyed hearing it. Kim can testify that ministry is birthed through misery. Through her loss and pain, rather than turning bitter toward God, the experience has refined her and made her more like Jesus…more than she will ever know.

Blessed be God, even the Father of our Lord Jesus Christ, the Father of mercies, and the God of all comfort; Who comforteth us in all our tribulation, that we may be able to comfort them which are in any trouble, by the comfort wherewith we ourselves are comforted of God. For as the sufferings of Christ abound in us, so our consolation also aboundeth by Christ. And whether we be afflicted, it is for your consolation and salvation, which is effectual in the enduring of the same sufferings which we also suffer: or whether we be comforted, it is for your consolation and salvation (2 Corinthians 1:3–6).

I was asked to speak at Ryan's funeral. The Scripture I shared with Kim, as I closed the service, is the same Scripture that strengthens her walk and resolve every day. She will never be totally free from the pain and loss down here, but she is promised a glorious day, when she and Ryan will meet again.

> *But now he is dead...can I bring him back again? I shall go to him, but he shall not return to me* (2 Samuel 12:23).

Kim, you have not allowed things to remain in your life that could rob you of the good God wishes to accomplish through you. Your life is producing beautiful fruit now. I have one more word for you... though actually it is not from me, but from our heavenly Father:

> *They that sow in tears shall reap in joy. He that goeth forth and weepeth, bearing precious seed, shall doubtless come again with rejoicing, bringing his sheaves with him* (Psalm 126:5–6).

Even though Kim may have had the wind knocked from her, she reached out and let the Lord touch her. Even though every day, she is reminded that life will no longer be the same, God has given her a new strength. Kim often refers to this as being "Ryan's story" but I tell her that because of the fruit now being produced in her life, this is "her story." Kim, you have found your Second Wind.

Local media has learned of Kim's foundation, "Pathways Of Hope," and she has been interviewed by local newspapers, and radio and television stations. If you want more information, or you just need prayer, you can contact:

Kimberly Bourgeois
Pathways of Hope
www.pathwaysofhope.com
Mamou, Louisiana

Chapter Sixteen

Mending Your Nets

So they signaled to their partners in the other boat to come and help
them. And they came and filled both the boats, so that they began to sink
(Luke 5:7 NKJV).

The story is told of three local pastors who all just happened to have
scheduled revival services for the same week. In keeping with their
Monday morning commitment to weekly fellowship, they met together
and the first pastor mentioned he'd had the best revival his church had
ever known—they had actually gained four new members. The second
pastor mentioned they had an even better revival as they had gained six
new members. Finally, the third pastor told the other two he had them
both beat. He admitted that though he had not taken in any new members, he did lose his ten biggest troublemakers.

Ministry often leaves men and women who serve Him broken,
ready to snap, and wishing there was something else to do! Before these
difficult times come (and they will), they had better have it settled in
their heart that they will never quit.

I will stand my watch and set myself on the rampart, and watch to see
what He will say to me, and what I will answer when I am corrected.
Then the Lord answered me and said: "Write the vision and make it
plain on tablets, that he may run who reads it. For the vision is yet for
an appointed time; but at the end it will speak, and it will not lie.
Though it tarries, wait for it; Because it will surely come, it will not
tarry (Habakkuk 2:1-3 NKJV).

Habakkuk was instructed to record what God had given to him because his motives were going to be questioned by others. If written down, it would not be as easy for him to lose his focus and change his course.

Lamentations 3:51 states that what I see with "my eye affects my heart." In my life and ministry, my God-given vision has kept me from disappointments that could have set me back, allowing me to focus on His presence and in seeing changed lives.

If a man is called to walk in an apostolic anointing, he will face apostolic tests. When these tests come, he must be determined that he will never quit. Jesus never gave those who crucified Him the satisfaction of thinking they had gotten the best of Him. Jesus showed Himself alive, conquering the grave, in spite of all He suffered.

> *The former account I made, O Theophilus, of all that Jesus began both to do and teach, until the day in which He was taken up, after He through the Holy Spirit had given commandments to the apostles whom He had chosen, to whom He also presented Himself alive after His suffering by many infallible proofs, being seen by them during forty days and speaking of the things pertaining to the kingdom of God* (Acts 1:1-3 NKJV).

When Jesus began building His team of disciples, He didn't look for those who never appeared to have a problem but for those who had every reason to quit but refused.

> *So it was, as the multitude pressed about Him to hear the word of God, that He stood by the Lake of Gennesaret, and saw two boats standing by the lake; but the fishermen had gone from them and were washing their nets. Then He got into one of the boats, which was Simon's, and asked him to put out a little from the land. And He sat down and taught the multitudes from the boat. When He had stopped speaking, He said to Simon, "Launch out into the deep and let down your nets for a catch." But Simon answered and said to Him, "Master, we have toiled all night and caught nothing; nevertheless at Your word I will let down the net." And when they had done this, they caught a great number of fish, and their net was breaking. So they signaled to their partners in the other*

boat to come and help them. And they came and filled both the boats, so that they began to sink (Luke 5:1-10 NKJV).

In this account, Jesus found an empty boat and tired fishermen. Even though they had fished all night, nothing could be produced to show for their labor. Yet their apparent failure was something that caught Jesus' attention. Jesus noticed though they were weary, and empty, they were washing their nets. There were some qualities inside these frustrated men that Jesus would need in people to whom He wished to impart the Kingdom.

Jesus found a boat that was empty and men who were willing to admit they had caught nothing which left them feeling like failures. Most men, when they feel like they have failed, simply quit. Rather than quitting, the weary fisherman used this opportunity to make the most of their time by washing their nets.

In the Greek, the word *pluo* means "washing." It also means "inspecting, mending, or repairing." The fishermen had caught nothing and were left feeling empty, ripped, and snagged. Although they had every reason to feel discouraged, their actions indicated they were preparing to go out and fish again. This attitude was the very thing that Jesus was looking for, the very kind of men He would trust with His Kingdom.

Things do not always go a man's way and may leave him feeling like a failure. When a man gives his best and things do not go as he had planned, he could question his call and be tempted to quit.

Personally, I must admit, not everything I do for the Kingdom or in the Kingdom produces a great harvest. Often the reward of my labor seems to be meager at best. I often say, "If it were easy, everybody would be doing it." I think of many men and women who have been disappointed while serving God. However, they keep praying, trusting God, and preparing to go and reach out to people all over again. The fishermen did not know the word "quit." In my own life, there are far more feelings of inadequacy than feelings of success, but I have learned to keep pressing on.

God cannot use me if I quit every time something does not go the way I would like it to go. God may not trust a man with success in ministry until he has been faced with an opportunity to quit, but doesn't.

What a pastor does, when he feels he has failed, reveals everything about him. When things do not go his way, when people walk out on him, when others walk away from him saying things that are not true, will he strike back? Will he quit? Or will he show by his actions that he will try again?

I often tell my congregation they need to see me tested or feeling like I failed. I do not mean failing morally or spiritually, but they need to see how I react to situations and to people when things do not go the way that I had planned. Will I keep my spirit sweet or will I turn vicious, depressed, vindictive, or hurtful? Will I begin blaming others? How can people have confidence in a man, trusting him with their lives, when he gives in to his emotions and crumbles under pressure?

On the other hand, I also remind my congregation that I need to see them tested. Not that I want to see them hurt or disappointed; but as their pastor, I need to know how they will react when things do not go their way. Will they get slack attending church? Will they point an angry fist at God? Will they point an accusing finger at me or blame others for their failure? We are in a battle, and as a pastor, I have to be able to trust those that carry my God-given vision.

Jesus needed to know whether or not the men He was connecting Himself to could become the Kingdom builders He needed. Would these men keep their composure under pressure or would they fall apart? Future success in ministry depends on the faithfulness of the ones to whom they are committed.

Jesus saw the boat on the shore and the fishermen as they finished washing their nets and asked if He could use their boat for a while. When the men agreed, Jesus had them push the boat out from the shore so He could speak to the people.

This must have been a humbling experience for the boat captain as Jesus, a total stranger, started giving instructions to him and his crew. Jesus' first command was to simply sit in shallow water. After a discourse to the people, Jesus turned to the fishermen, seeing they were able to take instructions, and told them to launch into deeper water.

Everyone must learn to sit in shallow water. Only then will they hear Him give the command to "launch out into the deep." God may not allow someone to venture into deeper water until it is clear that they can be trusted in the shallow. Once Jesus saw they could handle the loss of their pride and still follow instructions, He allowed them to catch such an enormous amount of fish that their nets began to break. It wasn't long until the call went out from the boat to those on the shore sitting idly in their own boat, to come quickly and help.

The harvest may begin with one man but could include others. Look at the other boat on the shore not being used. The ones who are ready to help a man may be the very same ones that once walked out on him. Everyone has people in their lives that may have once forsaken them. When people are abandoned for whatever reason, it usually makes them feel like quitting. The harvest may require that they still be included. The captain signalled to those that were on the shore, calling them "partners," and asked them to come and help. Those who have been hurt may have the opportunity to forgive those who are not on board with them and call them back into active duty.

At one point in my ministry, I was wrestling with the negative feelings of being walked out on. Feeling crushed, I had to let God rebuild my confidence and vision. I had to learn that only God could make my dreams come to pass. God let me experience failure so that He could take my dream and make it happen in such a clear way that I knew it was Him and not me. Because I chose to forgive, I found the ability to allow those who once hurt me to get back on board with my dream. These partners became a tremendous help in what was to come. Today, some of these partners remain my most trusted friends. It may be easier to retool an old partner than to find and learn to trust a new one.

God uses men to impact the lives of others, and in a difficult time, they may leave and never return. Some will never actually be back on the boat and involved in His particular ministry, but we can thank God that they are faithful somewhere. It is a testimony to the grace of God that the two ships were so filled with fish that both of them began to sink. When God starts to sink a man's ship, he can be confident that he is not going under. Help is on the way.

God often will not use a man until all of the flesh has been removed from him. In the words of Joseph, "Satan meant it for evil, but God meant it for good." The very test that causes someone to choose between being faithful or quitting may not actually be from the devil. His test may be sent from God to see if he is indeed a man He can trust with His Kingdom. The choice he will be facing may come as the result of someone who did him wrong or from circumstances beyond his control.

During our long-running revival, which began in 2004, a young lady named Amy, from Andrews, Texas, attended our services. She was in Houston to be at the bedside of her mother who was in the final stages of cancer. Amy often made the two-hour trip from the hospital to attend our revival services to request prayer for her mom. After her mother's death, when she was in Houston, she attended services and asked me to keep her father in prayer. Glenn Hammack was the pastor of a small church in Andrews. Still grieving over the loss of his wife, the church had all but dissolved around him as he tried to keep the church focused and going forward.

Though I had never met him, I made a habit of calling Pastor Hammack on a regular basis to pray and give him a word of encouragement. He shared with me that he and his wife had been praying for many years that revival would come to Andrews. While in prayer, God gave them a promise that a revival was in fact coming to Andrews. Pastor Hammack's wife was an intercessor, but she died before the promise came to fulfillment. I tried to get friends who were full-time evangelists to make the trip to West Texas, but they never seemed to be able to connect with the pastor. In hindsight now, I realize there was a work in Andrews that God wanted me to do.

An invitation was extended for me to go to Andrews and conduct revival services. I asked a pastor friend, Johnny Knight from Victoria, Texas, to assist me by leading worship, and intercessors joined with us for prayer support. When we arrived, we found the church had dwindled to only a very small handful of people, most of whom were Pastor Hammack's immediate family.

While struggling with the feelings that God must have made a bad mistake, Pastor Hammack and his family could have given up. It would have been easy to close the church and move on with their lives. In their brokenness, God showed up and brought beauty from the ashes. From the first service, a spirit of refreshing came and filled the sanctuary. The church was packed every night, and chairs had to be removed from the auditorium just to have a place to minister to all who came forward for prayer. Johnny Knight and I returned two months later to conduct another series of services. The people that were saved, restored, and healed became the nucleus for the work that God was beginning. What God was doing became the buzz of the town. When God began to move, everything changed. The church quickly outgrew their facility and was able to purchase the local cinema, renovating it into a beautiful church. Not only was the news spreading by word of mouth, but the local radio and television station aired reports and newspapers ran stories. The church is now out of debt and thriving. Because the church has known brokenness, it became a church with a heart, helping those who are hurting and in need.

The House of Mercy Ministries did experience an extended revival in 2009, running for twenty-two weeks. People drove to Andrews from across West Texas to be in the fertile atmosphere where so many miracles were taking place. Even though no evangelist was present, it wasn't necessary. When His presence comes, He is all you need. God did keep His promise to the Hammacks.

Several years later, God brought a very special woman into Pastor Hammack's life. She too had experienced tragedy in her own life, but she never gave up on God. Pastor Glenn Hammack and Mary Benner were married, and she has become a dynamic part of his life and ministry. House of Mercy Ministries continues to thrive as an oasis for His presence in this small West Texas oil town, all because God found a man, who although he was crushed, refused to quit.

Pastor Glenn Hammack and the congregation in Andrews are an inspiration for everyone who ever thought that their God-given dream was all but lost. They are living proof that God will keep His promises.

It must be understood that when God gives a man a vision, it must be tested. The means by which correction comes may be a family member, friend, foe, or a difficult situation. If he cannot handle the pressure of the test, he probably is not ready to handle the success that only comes through faithfulness.

When God gives a man a promise, the fulfillment of it may not be the next event to happen in his life. This is why it is important for the things God gives him to be recorded. When he is convinced he knows God's plan, he can run and not frustrate himself as to whether or not he is on track when he feels the urge to quit. He may ask himself one question, "Is my test worth it?" When a man has done all he can do, he can rest assured that God's promise to him will certainly come to pass—but only if he doesn't quit.

Chapter Seventeen

We Can't Even Help Ourselves

Let the righteous strike me; It shall be a kindness. And let him rebuke me; It shall be as excellent oil; Let my head not refuse it (Psalms 141:5 NKJV).

The story is told of an old bird who decided it no longer needed to fly south to avoid the horrible winters that northern states offered. He decided as tough as he was, he could easily brave the freezing cold temperatures of the cold North and avoid the three thousand mile flight to warmer weather.

It wasn't long after the weather began to change that he decided it wasn't a very good idea. While he was flying one day, the rain turned to ice and his wings were covered. He said, "This is the worst day of my life." As his wings grew heavy with accumulating ice, he discovered it was very difficult to fly. He looked down and saw an open barn door and decided it best to take shelter.

Once the bird was inside, the barnyard cow headed toward him. When she reached the bird, she stepped right over the top of him and dropped a warm plop down on top of his head. The old bird said, "This is without doubt the worst day of my life" since he had first almost frozen to death outside and then inside the barn was covered with a fresh, warm smelly plop. Soon he came to a new conclusion and said, "You know, it is starting to get nice and warm in here," and he began to sing. About the time he began to sing, the barnyard cat came in and heard the sound of a happy bird beneath the plop. In one swift swipe of its paw, the cat moved the plop, grabbed the bird, and ate it. End of story.

There are three morals to this story.

Moral number one: Just because someone drops a plop on you doesn't mean they are your enemy. I speak as a pastor who loves people and churches. I speak as an insider who loves them in spite of their imperfections. I will speak the truth in a way that is helpful. Just because I speak the truth doesn't mean I hate anyone.

Moral number two: Just because someone takes a plop off you, it doesn't mean they are your friend. There are pastors who will tell people what they want to hear so as to maintain their own level of comfort and not risk offending people.

Moral number three: When someone drops a plop on you, keep your mouth shut. When someone does speak the truth in love, we should listen, examine ourselves, and benefit from the words they say and grow from their advice. David said it like this:

Let the righteous strike me; It shall be a kindness. And let him rebuke me; It shall be as excellent oil; Let my head not refuse it (Psalms 141:5 NKJV).

A few years ago, Rachel and I decided to take a trip to Utah with two of our daughters for a week to visit a family member. One month after booking our flights, our plans changed and we were only able to spend a day in Utah. As we were scheduled to fly in and out of Las Vegas, we had to make a decision as to whether we wanted to stay there for an entire week. We did decide to take our trip as planned and had a very nice vacation. After arriving home, a preacher commented to me, "I wouldn't want to be caught in Vegas when Jesus comes." I thought to myself, *I wouldn't want to be caught in the house of God when Jesus comes.*

For the time is come that judgment must begin at the house of God (1 Peter 4:17).

Forty miles south of the church where I pastor, stands what used to be a church. This converted church paints a perfect picture of what happens when people lose a passion for the presence of God. It appears to me the congregation decided that winning souls and worshipping God were not profitable; they sold the building, and it was turned into a business that sold caskets. The new owners took the steeple off and replaced it with an open coffin to catch the attention of people driving by. The coffin remained on the roof until Hurricane Ike hit the Texas coast with winds in excess of a hundred miles per hour, blowing the coffin to the ground. Thankfully, the coffin was never returned to its place.

The Church, which Christ loves and gave His life for, has lost her way. It is the grace and mercy of the Lord that He is patient with her. The Old Testament prophet Hosea was commanded to marry a prostitute to demonstrate how a nation could lose their love for God.

When a church loses His presence, they will replace it with something that produces death. Many churches are no different than what Elisha found at Gilgal.

> *And Elisha returned to Gilgal, and there was a famine in the land. Now the sons of the prophets were sitting before him; and he said to his servant, "Put on the large pot, and boil stew for the sons of the prophets." So one went out into the field to gather herbs, and found a wild vine, and gathered from it a lapful of wild gourds, and came and sliced them into the pot of stew, though they did not know what they were. Then they served it to the men to eat. Now it happened, as they were eating the stew, that they cried out and said, "Man of God, there is death in the pot!" And they could not eat it* (2 Kings 4:38-40 NKJV).

In the above passage a hundred hungry prophets are found sitting at a table waiting for someone to tell them what to do and to bring them something to eat. There was a severe drought in the land, and no one had anything to bring to the table. The story is similar to the problems we see in America. How can churches help others when they themselves are the ones that need help?

The problem with America is not the White House; it is the Church House. The problem with America is not the President, the problem is the pastors. The reason the current President is reinterpreting our U.S. Constitution is because pastors are misquoting the Word of God. The reason Congress is at odds with the President is because the church boards are at odds with the pastors. Americans are cheating on their taxes because God's people are stealing His tithe. Married couples are falling out of love with each other and divorces are on the rise because Christians have lost their first love and are not committed to Christ. The reason there is a problem with homosexuality in America is because we haven't addressed it in the pew. The solution is to get the Church right, and America will follow. We should not be as worried about the state of the nation as we are the state of the Church.

The Church has lost His presence and has replaced it with things that will never satisfy. People think if they have the right music, a talented singer, a fiery preacher, or their favorite gifting that everything will be okay. The number one reason people never come back to church is because they have already been there. What the unchurched person finds in church is often not what it has been promoted to be. Members think His presence is there, but the person in need is the best person to answer that question.

I preached an illustrated message once where I did a spin-off of the old story, "The Emperor's New Clothes" where a couple of crooks convinced the king to purchase a beautiful robe that only "intelligent" people could see. To be perceived as being wise was more important to the advisors of the emperor than being honest and saying, "There is actually nothing there." The emperor decided that he should parade his new garments through town to display them to the common people. Again, no one wanted to be perceived as a fool so they pretended they too could see his beautiful new robe. The people were going along with it, although no one could actually see anything. Finally a young child spoke up and said, "He doesn't have anything on." The king, his advisors and all the people quickly realized, they were all actually fools. If the Church cannot see how she really is and help herself, how can she help others?

After Elijah sent the prophets out to look for food, one of them found something too good to be true right outside the door. If something has been passed by others, maybe it should not be embraced. With the right cook and the right spices, the stew appeared to be edible, but was soon found to be deadly. Just as the hungry prophets were willing to try anything, so has the Church. When will people realize that gimmicks aren't working? People want to see more than a motivational speaker or a hyped up music show with lights and smoke. People desire more than a state of the art facility. People just want to see Jesus.

An old preacher once said, "If you do not walk in your God-given authority, somebody else will, and they will use it against you." If a parent doesn't exercise authority in their home, the drug dealer on the street or the personality on television will influence the children. If a church doesn't provide an answer for the problems America is facing, someone else will, and they will use it against us.

> *And there came a man from Baalshalisha, and brought the man of God bread of the firstfruits, twenty loaves of barley, and full ears of corn in the husk thereof. And he said, Give unto the people, that they may eat* (2 Kings 4:42).

Baalshalisha was a Palestinian town that had Baal's name attached. Baal was a Philistine god and the word *shalisha* means "trouble" or "intense."

If the Church does not produce a solution to the trouble we are in, someone else will and use the answer against us. Because the prophets could not help themselves, the door was opened for someone of a different culture, a different tongue, a different dress, a different set of values, and most importantly, a different god from the one Israel served to offer something to sustain them. If the Church does not produce, she cannot complain about someone else who steps up to the challenge.

The Church has been given a mandate to heal the sick. When members are not practicing what Jesus commanded them to do, then someone needs to spring into action. Many people are forced to live in poverty, including elderly folks who have worked hard all their lives and now must spend everything they have in hopes of being healthy again.

God has put finances in the hands of believers to build churches, send missionaries, construct orphanages, and feed the hungry, but the funds are going into the hands of doctors. There is more than enough money to do all that His Church is expected to do, but the Church is broke, empty, and in need.

In 2010 in America, President Obama was able to pass legislation that would overhaul our healthcare system. While this bill was passed through the Senate, the Church was sitting on the solution. Jesus Christ has already paid for our healing through His precious blood. Imagine the thought that Christ's Body could save our nation billions of dollars if she would begin to practice what Jesus told her in the great commission.

People who adhere to some non-Christian religions often dress differently; talk differently; have different ideologies, laws, and philosophies from us; but most importantly, they serve a different god than we do. If the Church does not walk in her God-given authority, adherents to other religions may capitalize on her weakness and attempt to use it against her.

For decades, because of her love for God, America has been known as the "Light of the World." She still has that reputation, but some churches have begun to ordain homosexual and lesbian ministers. Alcohol misuse is rampant in Christians. Adultery is as common in the pew as outside the Church. No wonder some people of non-Christian religions feel they must rid the world of this "great Satan." The only solution for our national security could be the Church returning to true holiness.

For I say unto you, that except your righteousness shall exceed the righteousness of the scribes and Pharisees, ye shall in no wise enter into the kingdom of heaven (Matthew 5:20).

A revived Church that is true and holy is the only thing that can save America. How can the Church be glorious if His presence is not there? Thank God there seems to be a holy restlessness, and many of us believe that things are about to change.

Across America ministers have resorted to gimmicks and promotions to attract people to their churches. In reality, if churches would just give people what they are searching for, the hungry crowds could not be held back. When people find something in the house of God they can't find anywhere else, they will come. Many preachers present God as being one who is angry. Could it be if ministers had genuine compassion for souls, then sinners would respond to their message? The scriptures declare that people will not refuse salvation if they are shown the goodness of God. Romans 2:4 states that "the goodness of God leadeth thee to repentance."

I was invited to conduct a revival in a small town when a young lady walked in off the street and attended each of the services. It was obvious she was living a lesbian lifestyle and needed Jesus. Rather than being harsh, I extended to her the love of God, though she never came forward for salvation. The last night of the revival, I had a healing line and believed God for instant miracles for the people who came forward. By inspiration of the Spirit, I called for an elderly woman with a severe limp to come forward to receive ministry. I asked her to sit in a chair and then I asked this young lady to come forward and assist me, and she gladly accepted the offer. I asked her to help me by holding both the woman's feet in her hands and examine whether or not they were equal in length. She verified what I had already discovered: one leg was an inch and a half shorter than the other. As she continued to hold both feet in her hands, I began to minister to this woman, and as I spoke, we both saw her hips realign. The woman's leg was extended out to the equal length of the other one. Not only did the young lady see the miracle, she also felt it. Standing up promptly, she faced me and told me she was ready to give her heart to God.

Jesus used the healing ministry to gather a crowd so the gospel could be preached. Not only did He use it to become a beachhead for the gospel but to also show compassion to those who were hurting. Could it be if preachers ministered in the power of the Spirit, the way Jesus did, they would see the same results He saw? Jesus even promised Christians would do greater works than He.

And Jesus went forth, and saw a great multitude, and was moved with compassion toward them, and he healed their sick (Matthew 14:14).

Could the healing ministry be the greatest tool for evangelism given to the Church, and it is being overlooked? Healings have already been paid for and offered free to all. Because churches are not using what Jesus put in their hands, they are scratching their heads and wondering why people won't gather to listen to the message. May I suggest that the crowds can find entertainment at the theatre, comedy at the club, and competition on the ballfield? Why doesn't the Church offer something not found anywhere else—health and healing for all at the feet of Jesus?

What preacher has not preached on the twelve barrels of water in 1 Kings 18? Elijah gave instructions to pour the water over the sacrifice. The reason for the twelve barrels of water is that it was all they had left. People are too happy living on yesterday's experience. In this case, it had not rained in over three years, and the rivers were dry, and all they had left was what they had in the barrels. How old, stagnant, and bitter the precious water must have been.

Churches must admit what has been promoted has not worked and what has been presented does not satisfy. What is clung to is not life giving. Even though some methods might have worked yesterday, churches need to have a fresh revelation of His presence today. The Church must quit clinging to outdated ideas and methods that aren't working and pray for a fresh move of the Holy Spirit.

What would possess a man to dump out all the water they had? He must have known that rain was just over the horizon. Elijah could see what others could not see. He was drenched in something that he could not feel. The prophet was filled to overflowing with what had not yet fallen to the earth.

And Elijah said unto Ahab, Get thee up, eat and drink; for there is a sound of abundance of rain. So Ahab went up to eat and to drink. And Elijah went up to the top of Carmel; and he cast himself down upon the earth, and put his face between his knees, And said to his servant, Go up now, look toward the sea. And he went up, and looked, and said, There is nothing. And he said, Go again seven times. And it came to pass at the seventh time, that he said, Behold, there ariseth a little cloud out of the sea, like a man's hand. And he said, Go up, say unto Ahab, Prepare thy chariot, and get thee down, that the rain stop thee not. And it came to pass in the mean while, that the heaven was black with clouds and wind, and there was a great rain (1 Kings 18:41-45).

Some can hear the sound of an abundance of rain—it is okay to empty the barrels. Why doesn't the Church get ready for what God has already promised He would do? Running with our second wind will involve doing what Jesus commanded us to do in the great commission. When we do what we have never done, we will begin to see what we have never seen.

> *And they went forth, and preached every where, the Lord working with them, and confirming the word with signs following. Amen* (Mark 16:20).

Chapter Eighteen

Going Nuts

And he shall be like a tree planted by the rivers of water, that bringeth forth his fruit in his season; his leaf also shall not wither; and whatsoever he doeth shall prosper (Psalm 1:3).

Being an avid bow hunter, I spend a lot of time in the woods and have come to know trees quite well. I am always interested in the many Scriptures the Lord gave us comparing the righteous to trees, and how He wants us to flourish.

The righteous shall flourish like the palm tree: he shall grow like a cedar in Lebanon. Those that be planted in the house of the Lord shall flourish in the courts of our God. They shall still bring forth fruit in old age; they shall be fat and flourishing (Psalm 92:12–14).

And he shall be like a tree planted by the rivers of water, that bringeth forth his fruit in his season; his leaf also shall not wither; and whatsoever he doeth shall prosper (Psalm 1:1).

…that they might be called trees of righteousness, the planting of the Lord (Isaiah 61:3).

In 2011, here in Texas, we had our worst drought on record. Experts have said that 500 million trees died due to lack of moisture. This figure does not include the trees that perished from the four million acres destroyed by wildfires.

Foresters said the forest can and will replenish itself—if it would only rain. Rain does not provide an immediate impact; it can take ten to fifteen years for a forest to regrow, and it takes another ten to fifteen years for the trees to reach the age of maturity.

What often happens in the spirit realm can be reflected in the natural. In Scripture, times of famine usually followed a time when the heart of Israel had strayed. God would mirror what He was seeing in their lives back to them, through natural occurrences. As fresh water seems to be getting scarce, rivers are drying up, and glaciers appear to be melting, it makes you wonder if God is trying to tell us something today.

For we know that the whole creation groaneth and travaileth in pain together (Romans 8:22).

According to statistics from many denominations, church attendance and charitable giving are in decline. It is obvious that we have lost our moral compass. Many are saying that the Church is losing its influence, at least here in America. Look at a few statistics.

- There are 3,700 abortions that take place each day in America alone.
- One-third of all children actually born are born out of wedlock.
- Over half of all marriages are ending in divorce, and the divorce rate is as high inside the Church as outside of it.
- Many denominations in the United States are ordaining homosexual and lesbian clergy.
- Self-identified "Christians" have decreased from 86 to 76 percent in twenty years.
- In the last twenty years, self-professed atheists have risen from 1 million to 4 million.

The social indicators have recorded explosions in crime, violence, drug and alcohol abuse, school dropout rates, gang membership, and jail and prison populations.

In spite of all the facts and statistics that are discouraging, we know there is nothing wrong with God, His Gospel, or His Word. The Gospel is still working, just not in America and Europe, where the Gospel has been very strong in times past. There is revival in Asia, and most specifically, China. In Beijing, China's capital city, there are thousands of home churches with attendance ranging from sixty to one hundred. Local law enforcement is not concerned with them unless attendance exceeds one hundred.

There is revival in Africa. There are 85 million Pentecostal believers, and the church there is expanding at a rate of 4.5 percent annually, which is twice the natural birth rate. It is only a matter of time before the continent is fully Christianized.

There is a major revival taking place in Central and South America. The nation of Guatemala alone is over 50 percent Christian. Many other countries are becoming Christian, and there are millions of Brazilian believers.

The tide has turned in America and Europe, and now the world is sending their own missionaries to us. Europe has already been labeled "post-Christian," and because of the decline, many experts are beginning to say that America is quickly becoming post-Christian, as well.

This know also, that in the last days perilous times shall come. For men shall be lovers of their own selves, covetous, boasters, proud, blasphemers, disobedient to parents, unthankful, unholy, without natural affection, trucebreakers, false accusers, incontinent, fierce, despisers of those that are good, traitors, heady, highminded, lovers of pleasures more than lovers of God; having a form of godliness, but denying the power thereof: from such turn away (2 Timothy 3:1–5).

It appears that many Christians have other priorities than going to church or attending prayer meetings. Pastors are finding it harder to get people to remain committed. Fewer people are involved in outreach, and most Christians never share their faith.

The American church is in a drought, and the "trees" are dying. When trees start dying, we stand to lose a lot more than just trees. A large, mature tree actually produces its own mini-ecosystem, and it supports an entire range of life with its leaves and nuts. Birds, squirrels, deer, and other vegetation thrive when a tree is healthy.

Preparing for the 2011 deer hunting season, I spent a lot of time in the woods, and I saw the condition of the trees. They were in distress, and they did not offer much hope for the wildlife that depend on them. With the trees in this condition, it did not surprise me when the deer were skinny and appeared to be starving. When deer season began, I could have filled my deer tags, but I did not shoot any deer because they were so puny. Because of the drought and the condition of the trees, I didn't expect many deer could survive the coming winter. I could only imagine what lay ahead for the deer population.

During this record-breaking drought and the many wildfires, people were gathering together in prayer meetings and asking God to send rain. This is exactly the same thing churches that realize we need a revival to sweep America are doing. When there is a famine, the natural thing to do is to pray for rain. When people begin to pray, there is hope.

For there is hope of a tree, if it be cut down, that it will sprout again, and that the tender branch thereof will not cease. Though the root thereof wax old in the earth, and the stock thereof die in the ground; Yet through the scent of water it will bud, and bring forth boughs like a plant (Job 14:7–9).

Just as rain is the only thing that can save the trees, heartfelt prayer, with contrition and true repentance, is the only thing that can save America. If we pray, we know what the Lord has promised. Prayer brought rain and a national revival to Israel, and the same can happen for America.

And the Lord appeared to Solomon by night, and said unto him, I have heard thy prayer, and have chosen this place to myself for an house of sacrifice. If I shut up heaven that there be no rain, or if I command the locusts to devour the land, or if I send pestilence among my people; If my people, which are called by my name, shall humble themselves, and pray, and seek my face, and turn from their wicked ways; then will I hear from heaven, and will forgive their sin, and will heal their land (2 Chronicles 7:12–14).

When there is a famine and trees are dying, not only do you need rain, but you need trees to produce nuts to begin new trees. The strangest thing happened—about the time it appeared that all was lost, the oak trees produced a bumper crop of acorns, even though it had not rained. I have never seen so many acorns. The floor of the forest was covered, and everywhere I walked, my feet would crunch with the sound of acorns. The deer did not have to search for food because it was abundant.

While talking to a couple of old-timers, I mentioned this strange phenomenon. I learned that when a tree is in distress, it puts all of its remaining vigor into producing seeds in order to reproduce itself. Even a fruit tree, if it is distressed, will produce an unusual second harvest in the fall, in an all-out attempt to survive. After the acorns began to fall, I didn't see any more deer that season because they did not have to search for food, but I did see the fattest squirrels I have ever seen.

I want to be a Christian in a church that wins souls. I take my relationship with God and my job as a pastor seriously, but I have learned that I cannot put pressure on people to produce a harvest. A harvest will be produced when people genuinely fall in love with Jesus and begin sharing their faith with those around them.

I cannot put a guilt trip on people, but I can pray and ask the Father to let them fall in love with Him all over again. A man once said, "Let's pray like everything depends on God, and work as if everything depends upon us."

The fruit of the righteous is a tree of life; and he that winneth souls is wise (Proverbs 11:30).

Therefore said he unto them, The harvest truly is great, but the labourers are few: pray ye therefore the Lord of the harvest, that he would send forth labourers into his harvest (Luke 10:2).

America's only hope for survival is revival. It is time that we pray for God to send the much-needed rain. The Church needs to produce as many acorns as possible, and once He sends the rain, the nuts that have been produced and buried in fertile ground will take root and produce another forest. What I saw in the natural truly could be a reflection of what we are about to see in the spiritual. Until another mature forest is produced, "Let's All Go Nuts!"

Chapter Nineteen

Walking Out Your Promise

That ye be not slothful, but followers of them who through faith and patience inherit the promises (Hebrews 6:12).

In 1985, Rachel and I left the church in Saginaw, Texas, where we had served as youth pastors to pioneer the church we currently pastor in Corrigan. After our final service, Pastors F.J. and Lillie Pearce sat us down and gave us words of advice that I can never forget: "When things go right, give all the glory to God and don't let success go to your head, because it wasn't you; and when things go wrong, and you have done all He asked you to do, don't take it personally."

I knew this was good advice. This was one of the principles that led to the longevity of the Pearce's faithful service, spanning thirty-seven years at Saginaw Assembly of God. Many pastors and missionaries were called from under their ministry and are now serving God faithfully all over the world.

Life is not just about how a person handles success; it is also about how he deals with discouragement. Life is a journey, and during the course of a man's life, he will experience the highest highs and the lowest lows.

What could have been more exciting to Peter, James, and John than to end up on a mountain and see what no man had ever seen before? Who else could say that they had seen Jesus, Moses, and Elijah—all at the same place and moment in time? Peter was quick to suggest that three tabernacles should be erected, and they should just stay right where they were. Of course, that was not possible; there was work for them to do.

> *And after six days Jesus taketh Peter, James, and John his brother, and bringeth them up into an high mountain apart, And was transfigured before them: and his face did shine as the sun, and his raiment was white as the light. And, behold, there appeared unto them Moses and Elias talking with him. Then answered Peter, and said unto Jesus, Lord, it is good for us to be here: if thou wilt, let us make here three tabernacles; one for thee, and one for Moses, and one for Elias* (Matthew 17:1–4).

A few days later, at the Garden of Gethsemane, where Jesus often prayed, Peter was with Jesus and denied that he ever knew Him.

Don't give up on a man because of one thing he did wrong. Rather, stick with him because of all the things he did right. A single snapshot of his life could make it appear that everything was easy, while another snapshot could leave the impression that his life was very difficult. When a man begins walking out his promise, judge his life by his journey and not one of the single destinations.

Life is full of changes, and each one presents its own set of challenges. I often tell people, "If life is good, don't get too comfortable because it's going to change." Yet, with the same breath, I tell them, "If life seems unfair and cruel, don't quit because it too is going to change." How you handle success and deal with disappointment will determine the quality of your life.

God called Abraham out of his father's house, and gave him a promise that he had to walk out.

> *Now the Lord had said unto Abram, Get thee out of thy country, and from thy kindred, and from thy father's house, unto a land that I will shew thee: And I will make of thee a great nation, and I will bless thee, and make thy name great; and thou shalt be a blessing: And I will bless them that bless thee, and curse him that curseth thee: and in thee shall all families of the earth be blessed* (Genesis 12:1–3).

> *And the Lord said unto Abram. . .Lift up now thine eyes, and look from the place where thou art northward, and southward, and eastward, and*

westward: For all the land which thou seest, to thee will I give it, and to thy seed for ever. And I will make thy seed as the dust of the earth: so that if a man can number the dust of the earth, then shall thy seed also be numbered. Arise, walk through the land in the length of it and in the breadth of it; for I will give it unto thee (Genesis 13:14–17).

The promise to Abraham was big. The small part of the fulfillment that Abraham experienced during his lifetime made him the most prosperous man on earth. The promise continued through Isaac, Jacob, and Joseph. The scope of it was still being realized, and today, some five thousand years later, the promise is still coming to pass.

God also gave Moses the promise of what Israel should expect when they crossed the Jordan. It would unfold before them—not overnight, but only as they were able to inhabit the land.

And I will send hornets before thee, which shall drive out the [inhabitants] from before thee. I will not drive them out from before thee in one year; lest the land become desolate, and the beast of the field multiply against thee. By little and little I will drive them out from before thee, until thou be increased, and inherit the land (Exodus 23:28–30).

Joshua too had to walk out the promise after bringing Israel across the Jordan River. No promise from God is a "done deal"; it always has to be walked out.

Every place that the sole of your foot shall tread upon, that have I given unto you (Joshua 1:3).

You can tell much about the character of a man by the way he handles himself during the overall tenure of his journey. Too often pastors leave a church, or a spouse leaves a marriage, or someone quits a job during a difficult time. If people could hang on just a little bit longer, the problems they face would eventually seem as if they were nothing.

In my journey, thank God, I didn't quit when our church was in its infancy. Rachel and I know too well the feeling of being broken. During those challenging times, there were two reasons I didn't walk away. First, I didn't know how to quit. Pastors Paul and Patricia Emerson in Houston, Pastor Elmer and Dolly Weeks in Lufkin, and the Pearce's in

Saginaw, all may have eventually retired after long tenures as pastors, but they never quit. Second, God gave me a promise for my life, and I didn't want to abort the calling.

Ministry is about the ups and downs, the good times and the bad, happiness when new members join the church and frustration when disgruntled ones leave. I have experienced some of the best times, as well as the most difficult times, in the ministry. I know the feeling of being content where I am, or wishing there was something else I could do.

Before my church saw the wonderful move of God that began in 2004, we experienced a lot of changes. We were seeing an increase in the level of the presence of God, and we were preparing for greater things. In the middle of it all, we had some unpleasant challenges unlike anything I had ever encountered. It seemed we lost ground, and we had to rebuild major parts of the church leadership team. There were not enough adults to fill positions, so we used young teens. God did a work inside of us and prepared us again for what we knew would come to Corrigan and to East Texas.

I only share this information because it is something that all churches and pastors experience at least once in their lifetimes. I have enjoyed full restoration. I have no animosity of any kind, and many have again become very dear friends and valued members. Many were brought back into our lives to be a part of the revival that impacted so many.

Pastors whom I often minister to don't need to hear about my success and how I enjoyed my fruitful season of revival, as much as they need to hear about how I survived my challenges without becoming bitter or quitting the ministry. God, in His mercy, let me walk through some difficult times; but through it all, I received my promise. Now I can help pastors and churches prepare for their destiny even when it looks like all is lost.

I have also learned that even when things go well, you still lose people, but for Kingdom purposes. I thank God that people He impacted because of my ministry can go from here and be successful. But when they leave the nest, it always leaves a gaping hole that again has to be filled.

God touched young people, including my own children, in our

church. During the years leading up to the revival, and in the midst of it, I saw them become tremendous vessels. Their music, along with the team of other musicians and singers, and their gifts and talents helped usher in the presence of God during the extended revivals. Even though they were just teenagers, they became a wonderful part of my life.

Part of the price for success in ministry is not holding on to those who are like my own children, who have a Kingdom destiny. Though I loved them dearly, and they added value to my life, I had to learn to release them.

The day my daughter Heather left for college, my ministry changed. It was okay, though, because she had trained others to take her place. Those whom we poured ourselves in to, were also being prepared for ministry. When you lose those you have prepared for ministry, it is always bitter sweet. Seasons in my life change regularly because God is moving people up around me. I now understand the saying well, "The more things change, the more they stay the same." I have learned the promise God gives is bigger than any one person, and you must keep walking it out.

Like Peter, James, and John, who offered to build three tabernacles, I did everything in my power to keep the team intact. But I cannot remain there, nor can I hold others there. God has a huge work going on, and we all have a part to play in it. If I refuse to turn loose of those who are prepared to receive their own promise, I am robbing another person of the joy of rising up and receiving their own promise. I have found that God brings wonderful people into my life for a season. In the words of Solomon, "To every thing there is a season, and a time to every purpose under the heaven" (Ecclesiastes 3:1).

My church does not have the same makeup of personalities it had a few years ago. Today there are many new faces and some new and different giftings. God is preparing us for our next wave.

You can only get to your destiny by continuing on. I have determined that my fellow-laborers in ministry, my congregation, and my family will never see me quit. In the words of Paul, "I was not disobedient unto the heavenly vision" (Acts 26:18). I thank God that He chose who I walked behind in ministry, leaving me an example to follow.

I mentioned in chapter fifteen that I have a great relationship with the pastor in Mamou, Louisiana. I called and told him I had a word from the Lord, but on this particular occasion, I knew he had heard me, but he did not say anything other than that he would get back with me. Several months passed and I finally received a call from him. His words were, "Didn't you tell me you had a word for Mamou?" I said I did and asked him when I could bring it. I didn't know it then, but it would be an important "on time" word. It is obvious now, this whole event, and the word I was to deliver, was orchestrated by the Lord.

Revival services began that week on Sunday night and were scheduled to run through Tuesday. The first night I preached a message that was titled "Walking Out Your Promise," and it involved the subject I am sharing in this chapter. I thought it meant something when I preached it then. I know it means something now.

I shared in this message that life is about changes. You must endure the difficult times and walk through the good times. Sometimes we are thrust forward, and sometimes it feels like we are set back. On this occasion, I told the church that when change comes, all we can do is to keep our eyes on Jesus and keep walking forward.

Raymond LaFleur was the worship leader, but he had been very sick my first visit to Mamou. Raymond was present, but the church had to rely on recorded CDs to provide worship for them because they had no musicians. Raymond recovered and at the second revival I conducted there, he was leading worship. He had family members playing in the band beside him, and he was in full stride. These were glorious days in the church and the music with the Cajun flair could be heard, resonating up and down the city streets of Mamou. The music always brought the atmosphere of heaven to where we were, and the services always ended with the men stacking the folding chairs against the wall, and the whole church came alive with dancing and rejoicing.

On this particular Monday night, the night after I preached the message "Walking Out Your Promise," Raymond walked into the church, and my wife noticed how his face seemed to be glowing. As he came in, he turned to his son and held his thumb and forefinger about an inch apart, then said, "I'm about this close to dying." His brother, who was the pastor, said, "Brother, do you feel like singing tonight?" Raymond replied, "If I die, I will die doing what I enjoy, praising the

Lord." Raymond turned to his sister, Rebecca LaFleur, and said, "Sister, if I don't finish this song, you just go ahead and finish it for me."

The service began, and Raymond led us in worship. About the third song for the evening, Raymond began to sing, "When the Savior Reached Down for Me." When he got to the part of the chorus that said, "When He reached way down for me," I saw Raymond turn to his sister, grinning from ear to ear and cradling his guitar in his arms. He then leaned back against the wall and slid down it, until he was in a sitting position, and suddenly he was gone from this life. Death for Raymond was a beautiful experience. Everyone knew that Heaven was in the house that night.

For the church in Mamou, Raymond's death came as a shock. The Lord sent me there the night before to prepare them because the season was about to change. The music may never be like it was when Raymond was there. But the church moves on and thrives.

Do not redirect the course of your life because things are not what you expected them to be. Remember this scripture and take it to heart:

> *That ye be not slothful, but followers of them who through faith and patience inherit the promises. For when God made promise to Abraham, because he could swear by no greater, he sware by himself, Saying, Surely blessing I will bless thee, and multiplying I will multiply thee. And so, after he had patiently endured, he obtained the promise* (Hebrews 6:12–15).

I believe your best is yet to come. Press on through what you may be going through and obtain the promises of God. The man who walks with the Lord will always reach his destination. Every time life presents a challenge you are not ready for, don't let it set you back. Pick yourself up, shake the dust off, and prepare to walk out your promise, with your second wind.

Chapter Twenty

When He Closes the Book

We spend our years as a tale that is told (Psalm 90:9).

A person's life may be identified by their occupation, something they invented or a great accomplishment. Unfortunately, others may have their life defined by their medical challenges, poor choices they once made, or the things that did not go as planned. A church, as well, may be defined by impacting a city, a breakthrough revival, or a great achievement, but most often it is remembered by a split among the membership, the failure of a leader, or something that went wrong. More often than not, identification comes from the challenges one has faced, rather than the accomplishments one has achieved.

In Mark 5, we read of a man who will always been identified as the man who lived in the tombs. Even though the Lord delivered him from unclean spirits, which had led him to vile and abusive behavior, he is rarely mentioned as the man whom Jesus delivered.

And they came over unto the other side of the sea, into the country of the Gadarenes. And when he was come out of the ship, immediately there met him out of the tombs a man with an unclean spirit, Who had his dwelling among the tombs; and no man could bind him, no, not with chains: Because that he had been often bound with fetters and chains, and the chains had been plucked asunder by him, and the fetters broken in pieces: neither could any man tame him. And always, night and day, he was in the mountains, and in the tombs, crying, and cutting himself with stones (Mark 5:1–5).

The tormented man had lived a wretched life, driven by negativity. He could not be civilized, clothed, or bound. He spent his life crying, day and night, living among the tombs. The disrespect he had for himself led to his own self-destructive behavior. He would never get any help, living where he was living among the tombs; such is the case of people who dwell there.

The only contacts the demonized man had with other people were with those grieving over their own losses. Monuments were added on a daily basis, reminding him that dreams never turn out the way people had hoped and every epitaph was set in stone. Jesus and His disciples landed on the shore close to the tombs, but they had a different purpose for being there than burying their dead. A confrontation between darkness and light was about to be witnessed, and the man bound all of his life was about to be set free.

I mentioned in chapter fifteen that a fig tree does not have the ability to shake a coon from it; neither does a man have the ability for his own liberation from demonic torment. Everyone needs an outsider to set them free from chains and mind-sets that have them bound, from the abuse they have suffered at the hands of others, or the results of poor decisions they may have made in their own life.

Because of everything he had been through, the man living in the tombs felt death was preferable to life. He chose to hang around with the constant reminder that things always go wrong and nothing ever goes right.

While people are living in tombs, though not meaning to, they are actually immortalizing their disappointments and hurts, which then lead to unforgiveness and bitterness. People feel imprisoned and are convinced there is no way to change their situation.

But when he saw Jesus afar off, he ran and worshipped him...(Mark 5:6).

When Jesus comes, He will reclaim what belongs to Him. Anyone or any church can have a change of identity. The only way you will have change is when you welcome His presence into your life. There will be a happy ending to every story when people allow Jesus into their predicament. Jesus will never leave things the way He found them. Jesus took authority over the negativity and drove out the possessed man's source of trouble, and the outlook instantly changed.

Jesus gave them leave. And the unclean spirits went out (Mark 5:13).

Jesus is able to turn around any situation that has spiraled out of control, leaving a person depressed and confused. He can also turn around a burned out pastor who is ready to quit or breathe new life into a church which has lost its passion and felt they have gone as far as they can go. Jesus will always close the book on failure if you let Him. When He closes the book, He will open a new book with a brand new destiny.

Jesus began His earthly ministry by declaring things needed to change. On a day when Jesus entered the synagogue, He was given a scroll, and He immediately turned to Isaiah and began to read:

And when he had opened the book, he found the place where it was written, The Spirit of the Lord is upon me, because he hath anointed me to preach the gospel to the poor; he hath sent me to heal the broken-hearted, to preach deliverance to the captives, and recovering of sight to the blind, to set at liberty them that are bruised, To preach the acceptable year of the Lord. **And he closed the book** (Luke 4:17–20 author emphasis).

The prophet Isaiah expounded on the passage from which Jesus quoted, "To appoint unto them that mourn in Zion, to give unto them beauty for ashes, the oil of joy for mourning, the garment of praise for the spirit of heaviness" (Isaiah 61:3).

I often tell people when I pray with them, "The devil never should have messed with you," and "Your test is being turned into a testimony and your mess into a message." When people welcome the presence of Jesus, they will experience a radical transformation. For the man living in the tombs, his life would never be the same. People who had known this man all of his life could not believe what they had seen the Lord do.

And they came to Jesus, and see him that was possessed with the devil, and had the legion, sitting, and clothed, and in his right mind (Mark 5:15).

Too often people, even churches, hang on to things that went wrong and are either unable or unwilling to turn loose of it and simply get over it. Often, people are not even aware that help is available. Individuals, and even entire churches, should release things that have brought them pain or that have not gone right, which has brought them their identity.

Nothing is too hard for the Lord. I have written this book to help others prepare for what is needed most—a fresh move of God. When times are tough and the "trees" are dying, we do not need more gimmicks, nor should we continue on with things that have not worked. The thing we need more than anything is the presence of the Lord to return to our lives and churches. Not only is His presence the only hope for people and congregations, but it is also the only hope for America and the nations of the world.

The Lord is pleading. He is knocking at our door, like the man who stood at the door but whose wife was comfortable and cozy in her warm bed, pondering her decision to arise and let her husband in. Jesus will not tarry long. If we are not interested in His presence, He may withdraw Himself.

The priests said not, Where is the Lord? and they that handle the law knew me not: the pastors also transgressed against me, and the prophets prophesied by Baal, and walked after things that do not profit. Wherefore I will yet plead with you, saith the Lord, and with your children's children will I plead (Jeremiah 2:8–9).

There are those who are too busy and are not willing to do things to accommodate Him. However, there are others of us who are looking for our day of visitation. We are not just sitting idly by and waiting for Him to "show up"; we are aggressively doing the things He is attracted to. Some of us will do anything to get His attention. Those who have lost their passion for His presence do not understand those of us who are desperate. Because we know there is coming a revival of global proportions, we are doing all we can to prepare to receive what He has already promised He would do.

You and I may appear to be hidden from the world in small, out-of-the-way places, but He knows where we are. We may think we know, but we don't really know who we are and what He is doing inside of us. For now, we are hidden from the mainstream of the world while He prepares us. To this point, it has not been our time, and we realize that "waiting time is not wasted time." We are about to receive our mandate and be told it is time to shine. The veil will be removed from the eyes of those who have doubted and misunderstood us. The world will begin to say, "Where did all of these empowered Christians, who are walking in the Spirit of God and His authority, come from?"

The book is being closed on situations that have left us feeling in-significant, like we have failed or have accomplished little. His presence is coming back and we are rising up, preparing to run with our second wind.

We all need to be filled with His Spirit. When we do, we will walk in His power and discover new and wonderful gifts He is making avail-able—the very gifts needed that will bring in an unprecedented harvest of souls. People will not be drawn into the Kingdom only by popular ministries and large churches but by common, ordinary people like our-selves, walking in God's glory. It is clear, the Church is God's agency to bring in this last days harvest. The Lord is restoring health to His Body.

God is breathing new life back into the pastors who were once on the verge of quitting. Some who may have already quit are about to be called back into active duty. Many disheartened laborers are about to learn to ride His horse.

Church, get ready! The winds are shifting, the tide is turning, the current is rising, and we are about to experience the greatest move of God the world has ever seen—a revival of global proportions. This is about to be the Church's finest hour. Are you ready to start "Running with Your Second Wind"?

About the Author

Phil Corbett knew the calling of God on his life at the age of five. When he was twelve, his pastor took him to the small East Texas town of Corrigan to tear down an abandoned church. Phil helped him by pulling nails and stacking lumber. As a result of this experience, God spoke to his heart to one day go back and build a church.

In 1985, Phil, and his wife, Rachel, moved to Corrigan, to pioneer First Assembly of God. After several years of minimal results in ministry, he began to realize there must be more. Frustrated with hearing success stories from other church leaders and planters, he prayed a very simple prayer that changed his life. That prayer was this, "I am so tired of hearing the stories that belong to someone else, would You please give me some stories of my own?"

Phil learned that hunger for God must precede the things that happen only in His Presence. God took him on a spiritual journey that forever changed his life. This journey began at the Brownsville Assembly of God revival in Pensacola, Florida. After experiencing encounters with God in the services there, God revealed to Phil that if he wanted to experience personal revival in his own life and ministry, he too would have to do the things that would attract the Presence of God.

After experiencing a season of revival in his own church, he soon had his own stories to tell. In 2003 First Assembly of God began a revival that was scheduled to last for three days, but God had other plans and the services went on for many weeks. The next year, God showed up again during a revival in which the heavens opened up over Corrigan, and services continued for the next eighty-eight weeks. During this time of revival, people traveled to this small town from all over the United States and many different nations. People from all walks of life went down the aisle for salvation, and scores of those attending were healed.

The congregation releases Pastor Phil to take this message of revival and healing to churches in the United States and internationally. He believes that the best days of the Church are ahead, and that God is mobilizing believers around the world to walk out their God-given destinies in power. His ministry is named "Second Wind Ministries" and is a source of encouragement to pastors and other church leaders who may be feeling frustrated or burned out.

An additional dimension of his ministry is in the area of divine healing and miracles. Phil believes that healing the sick is not only the mandate of the Church, but that it is also one of the greatest tools for evangelism. Romans 2:4 says, "It is the goodness of God that leads men to repentance."

Phil and his beautiful wife Rachel were married in 1982 and are very active in the ministry together. They have been blessed with four lovely daughters (Amy, Bethany, Heather, and Jessica), four wonderful sons-in-law (David, Mark, Joe, and William), and one beautiful grand-daughter, Chloe.

Author Contact Information

Pastor Phillip Corbett
Second Wind Ministries
(936) 398-2235

Email: pastor@corriganfirst.org
Website: runningwithyoursecondwind.com
Facebook: Second Wind Ministries

First Assembly of God
1700 North Home
Corrigan, Texas 75939